Designing and Using
PERFORMANCE TASKS

For my late parents, Richard and Patricia Flach.
The writing of this book represents lessons learned from each of you.

Designing and Using
PERFORMANCE TASKS

Enhancing Student
Learning and Assessment

TRACEY K. SHIEL

CORWIN
A SAGE Publishing Company

FOR INFORMATION:

Corwin

A SAGE Company

2455 Teller Road

Thousand Oaks, California 91320

www.corwin.com

SAGE Ltd.

1 Oliver's Yard

55 City Road

London, EC1Y 1SP

United Kingdom

SAGE Pvt. Ltd.

B 1/I 1 Mohan Cooperative Industrial Area

Mathura Road, New Delhi 110 044

India

SAGE Publications Asia-Pacific Pte. Ltd.

3 Church Street

#10–04 Samsung Hub

Singapore 049483

Acquisitions Editor: Jessica Allan

Associate Editor: Kimberly Greenberg

Editorial Assistant: Katie Crilley

Production Editor: Veronica Stapleton Hooper

Copy Editor: Judy Selhorst

Typesetter: Hurix Systems Pvt. Ltd.

Proofreader: Lawrence Baker

Indexer: Judy Hunt

Cover Designer: Michael Dubowe

Marketing Manager: Lisa Lysne

Printed in the United States of America

Library of Congress Cataloging-in-Publication Data

Names: Shiel, Tracey, author.

Title: Designing and using performance tasks : enhancing student learning and assessment / Tracey K. Shiel.

Description: Thousand Oaks, California : Corwin, a SAGE Company, 2016. | Includes bibliographical references and index.

Identifiers: LCCN 2016019832 | ISBN 9781506328720 (pbk. : alk. paper)

Subjects: LCSH: Competency-based education—United States. | Educational tests and measurements—United States.

Classification: LCC LC1032 .S55 2016 | DDC 371.26—dc23 LC record available at https://lccn.loc.gov/2016019832

This book is printed on acid-free paper.

SFI Certified Sourcing
www.sfiprogram.org
SFI-00453

16 17 18 19 20 10 9 8 7 6 5 4 3 2 1

Contents

Note from the Publisher: The author has provided web content in Chapter 5 which is available to you through QR Codes. To read a QR Code, you must have a smartphone or tablet with a camera. We recommend that you download a QR Code reader app that is made specifically for your phone or tablet brand.

List of Figures
and Tables

Acknowledgments

The process of writing a book is daunting, but the completion of the book is so rewarding that it makes the challenges along the way worth the effort. There are certain people who deserve to be acknowledged, as each and every one of them has had an impact on me as I've worked to complete this book.

First and foremost, I need to thank my loving husband, John. He was witness to me writing my first book, but this one was very different and required a different approach. John tolerated our having to turn down opportunities to meet with friends, or to go out to dinner, and we even postponed a trip to Hawaii. This book would have not come to fruition if it were not for his support and understanding throughout the process, and his enabling me to take the time I needed to write it.

Early in the process, I had a few meltdowns as I wrapped my head around how to approach this book, and a few rants may have ended up on Facebook. In particular, I need to thank Dr. Angela Peery for setting me straight, responding to questions, sharing writing advice, and overall being a good friend. I could always count on Angela responding to me through Facebook Messenger just when I needed a little nudge to keep me moving forward.

I have to thank a few particular educators at W. Reily Brown Elementary School in Dover, Delaware. First is Dr. Susan Frampton, who arranged for me to present an initial process to a handful of her staff last summer; based on their feedback, I was able to refine the process. Additionally, once I had refined the process, Michelle Caulk and Emily Peterson, with the support of Monica McCurry, were able to write a performance task using the template and use it with students. Both Michelle and Emily shared written reflections with me and provided a few student products that are included in Appendix 1. They took a leap of faith in employing the template and the process, and I am very thankful for all they did as busy classroom teachers.

The process for writing a performance task presented in this book is different from that in my first book, *Engaging Students Through Performance Assessment* (Flach, 2011), as a result of my learning and professional growth. In particular, a lot of *visible learning* concepts are embedded in the process discussed here, and I want to thank several people who are connected to visible learning who had email exchanges with me that helped to clarify my understanding and application of the concepts to the performance task development process. These include Dr. John Hattie, Jayne-Ann Young, Kristin Anderson, Dr. John Almarode, and Pam Hook. My thanks to all of you for responding to my emails seeking clarification and understanding, so I could incorporate some of the best aspects of visible learning into the process for developing and using performance tasks to deepen student learning and application. A thank-you also goes to my friend Josh McCarthy, a winemaker by trade and a technology wizard who rescued me after I attempted to re-create the effect size "barometer." All of you helped my thinking to come together.

A special thank-you goes to Jerome Sanchez, a deputy sheriff with the Erie County Sheriff's Department in New York. Jerome was a seventh-grade student at the Wellsville Middle School during my first year as a social studies teacher (1990–1991), when I experimented with a version of performance tasks in my classroom. Through Facebook, I reconnected with Jerome a few years ago, and in December 2015, I reached out to him to find out what he remembered about my social studies classroom. He sent me a response, which I received a day before my birthday, that I will never forget—it brought tears to my eyes. Thank you, Jerome, for sharing how I affected your life; your note made my years as a teacher worthwhile. I can only hope that other teachers realize the importance of teacher–student relationships, so that they understand that they can take the risk of using performance tasks in the classroom without mayhem breaking out.

Finally, this book would not be possible were it not for Corwin and all of its wonderful staff. A second thank-you needs to go to Kristin Anderson for believing in me and the topic of performance tasks and encouraging me to submit a proposal for consideration. Dan Alpert and Jessica Allan are the two Corwin editors I worked with throughout the process, and I am very appreciative of their understanding of my personal circumstances as I worked on this book. The editors are the ones who bring the book to life, and their importance cannot be overlooked. A particular thank-you to Jessica for tolerating my numerous emails and providing her wisdom and support to help me finalize this book.

My thanks to each and every one of you who played some role in my writing this book. I can only hope that it has as much of an impact on teachers and administrators as you had on me as I was writing it, so that students can reap the benefits of challenging and engaging learning.

Publisher's Acknowledgments

Corwin wishes to acknowledge the following peer reviewers for their editorial insight and guidance.

Perri Anne Bentley
Grade 3 Teacher
Ballentine Elementary School
Varina, North Carolina

Cathy Bonneville Hix
Supervisor of K–12 Social Studies
Arlington Public Schools
Arlington, Washington

Dr. Leslie Hitchens
Peer Assistance and Review Consulting Teacher
Saint Paul Public Schools
Saint Paul, Minnesota

Pamela L. Opel
Teacher
Gulfport School District
Gulfport, Mississippi

Michelle Strom
Middle School Language Arts Teacher
Fort Riley Middle School
Fort Riley, Kansas

Dr. Ann M. Yanchura
Literacy Coach
Forest Hill Community High School
West Palm Beach, Florida

About the Author

Tracey K. Shiel has been in the field of education for more than 25 years, in several positions, including teacher, principal, school business administrator, assistant superintendent for curriculum and instruction, and interim superintendent. She holds a bachelor's degree in economics from the University of Richmond, a master's in reading education from Syracuse University, and a certificate of advanced study in educational administration from the State University of New York in Oswego. She has been an educational consultant in some capacity since 2005, providing educational services nationally and internationally, focusing on instruction, assessment, leadership coaching, and implementation. She is currently an author/consultant for Corwin and is a certified presenter for seminars on visible learning. Through her company, Thought Partners, Tracey provides research-based educational services, including leadership coaching, professional development, implementation planning and execution support, and special project educational services of the highest quality, to support and develop educational leaders' ability to lead classrooms, schools, and districts to superior academic performance. As a skilled communicator, she is adept at facilitating the development of implementation success action plans to achieve critical educational goals.

Tracey was initially certified as a leadership performance coach, and she has also been certified as a hallmarks educational coach. She has provided leadership coaching to administrators for state departments of education, district administrators, building administrators, and instructional coaches to support the achievement of critical projects as well as to develop their leadership capacity and that of those around them. Currently, Tracey is refining her own leadership coaching model, balanced educational leadership coaching, which melds coaching techniques with mentoring and consulting components.

Tracey retains a passion for classroom instruction and assessment, specifically nonfiction reading and writing instructional strategies and performance tasks. She is well versed in the Common Core State Standards, which emphasize her passions. Tracey is the author of *Engaging Students Through Performance Assessment: Creating Performance Tasks to Monitor Student Learning* (2011), which incorporates Common Core examples throughout. She brings a wealth of real-world experience, researched-based knowledge, and attention to detail to her presentations, coaching, and implementation support, providing powerful educational services to her clients. As principal Dr. Susan Frampton has stated in reference to Tracey's coaching: "My work with Tracey Shiel has benefited my staff, community, and most importantly my students. Well versed with current research and the ability to effect change, Tracey supports me by asking the difficult questions that challenge my thinking. A guide, Tracey helped me clearly assess where we are as a school, plan where we are going, and monitor our progress. My work with Tracey gets results for my students and provides me with a safety net when the going gets tough."

Tracey Shiel can be reached at traceyshiel@corwinlearning.net.

Introduction

Education is not the filling of a pail, but the lighting of a fire.

—W. B. Yeats

When I think of my own 13 years of K–12 education, I realize that most of my learning experiences were the "filling of the pail," with only an occasional "lighting of a fire." Most of my learning experiences involved sitting in rows of seats, listening to the teacher, and independently completing worksheets. The learning experiences I remember that would fall into the category of "lighting of a fire" include bringing our cat Fluff to school for show-and-tell in first grade; sewing together a patchwork apron with pink, blue, and flowered patches; creating an ink drawing of a forest that was published in the middle school arts publication *Black on White*; constructing a six-bottle wine rack for my parents; writing a research paper on mountain lions; dissecting a frog; writing a research paper on Reaganomics and the "trickle-down effect"; and writing a poem using alliterative verse after reading *Beowulf*. In all of these cases, I was either learning through application or demonstrating what I had learned through application. This is the essence of performance tasks, the application of knowledge and skills. What learning experiences from your K–12 years of education do you remember favorably? How do they compare to mine?

Standards: Then and Now

With the 2016–2017 school year, the educational standards movement in the United States came full circle. The movement started as a responsibility of the individual states in the 1990s, and by 2010 the federal government stepped in and pressured states to adopt certain standards, specifically the Common Core State Standards (CCSS), as a condition of applying for Race to the Top grant funds. With the passage of the Every Student Succeeds Act at the end of 2015, the standards that students need to attain were once again up to each state. Just to bring all readers up to speed, since there is a growing influx of new and younger teachers as baby boomers retire, I offer below a brief history of the standards movement. The standards are at the core of all performance tasks, and if we truly want every student to succeed, we need high-quality standards for students to attain.

History of the Standards Movement

A year after I graduated from high school, the National Commission on Excellence in Education published *A Nation at Risk* (1983), which asserted that the U.S. education system was plagued with "mediocrity" and had lost sight of the "high expectations and disciplined effort" needed to provide a high-quality and enriching education. That research paper was the trigger for a series of educational innovations, initiatives, political policies, and laws, all intended to improve the quality of education in the United States. As a result of the Improving America's Schools Act of 1994, which was the reauthorization of the Elementary and Secondary Education Act of 1965, the standards movement began. States individually created and adopted grade-span (K–2, 3–5, 6–8, 9–12) standards and conducted assessments in grades 4 and 8 and once in high school (Flach, 2011).

Then, on January 8, 2002, under the watch of President George W. Bush and Secretary of Education Rod Paige, No Child Left Behind (NCLB) was signed into law, and the Age of Accountability was born. Periodic assessments were now replaced with grade-specific assessments in math and reading for grades 3–8 and one assessment in high school. The birth of adequate yearly progress (AYP) occurred with NCLB, all in the name of closing the achievement gap between Caucasian students and their African American, socioeconomically disadvantaged, English language learner, and special education counterparts. If a school failed to meet AYP for two or more years, it was forced to implement a series of measures that were intended, in the eyes of the federal government, to support the school (Klein, 2015). The measures, however, were more punitive than helpful. This was accountability in action.

The American Recovery and Reinvestment Act of 2009 was signed into law by President Barack Obama, and Secretary of Education Arne Duncan was the mastermind behind the Race to the Top grants funded by the act, which were intended for state education departments. States needed to address four priorities in their applications in order to be considered for Race to the Top grants, and one of those priorities was adopting the Common Core State Standards, which were in the process of being developed (U.S. Department of Education, n.d.). The Race to the Top grants enticed states to adopt the standards in hopes of filling their education coffers, as funds were being depleted as a result of the recession that started in 2008. Initially, only 44 states and territories adopted the CCSS (Flach, 2011).

During the 2014 and 2015 school years, there was a lot of turmoil over the Common Core State Standards as well as the Next Generation Assessments (created by the Smarter Balanced Assessment Consortium and the Partnership for Assessment of Readiness for College and Careers), which went online in the spring of 2015 to measure student progress on the CCSS. Numerous articles were published in both educational journals and news outlets, some criticizing and others promoting the CCSS and the Next Generation Assessments. Parents started to rise up against the Next Generation Assessments by opting their children out of taking the tests and urging other parents to do the same. The CCSS and the Next Generation Assessments were running into problems across the country as parents began organizing and states began to reconsider the adoption of the CCSS. Luckily, the Elementary and Secondary Education Act of 1965, which was the grounding legislation for all of the subsequent acts, was up again for reauthorization, and by midsummer Congress was closing in on a final agreement. It could not have occurred at a better time.

The Standards Now

On December 10, 2015, President Obama signed into law the Every Student Succeeds Act (ESSA), reauthorizing the Elementary and Secondary Education Act of 1965. The touted coup for the legislation is that it relinquishes a fair amount of the federal government's control over the states and diminishes the role of the U.S. Department of Education. It is not clear yet how much control will truly be relinquished, but the pendulum is swinging back to the states having more control and decision-making powers concerning education, including standards and assessments (Klein, 2016). Thus, it will be up to state legislatures and state departments of education to make decisions that will focus education on student learning, embracing teachers and administrators as the professionals they are rather than instituting demoralizing legislation that penalizes instead of supports them. States still must retain high standards, but they do not have to be the CCSS—this freedom is a key piece of the 2015 legislation.

Even though Ohio, Missouri, and Maine abandoned the CCSS before the adoption of ESSA, states should not make hasty decisions on the CCSS. The standards were developed to meet certain criteria, which they have largely achieved. As the Common Core State Standards Initiative (n.d.) states on its website, the standards are:

1. Research- and evidence-based

2. Clear, understandable, and consistent

3. Aligned with college and career expectations

4. Based on rigorous content and application of knowledge through higher-order thinking skills

5. Built upon the strengths and lessons of current state standards

6. Informed by other top performing countries in order to prepare all students for success in our global economy and society

If the CCSS meet all these criteria, what are the reasons to change from the CCSS and spend time and money at the state level to develop a different set of standards or revert to previous state standards?

An Opportunity for Change

There is currently an opportunity for states and their departments of education to reflect on the significant changes that have occurred over the past few decades and learn from those experiences. Accordingly, in the 2016–2017 school year, some states transitioned to new standards, with full implementation of these plans to take place in the 2017–2018 school year (National Conference of State Legislatures, n.d.).

At no other time in education have we known more than we do now about what works *best* in schools, as well as how the brain learns. We have the research to support what works best, so what is preventing schools and districts from acting on this knowledge and making the changes that are necessary to close the achievement gap and promote student progress and growth for all students? The most influential research in this area has been conducted by

Dr. John Hattie and published in his book *Visible Learning* (2009), which will be elaborated in Chapter 1. Hattie has applied his research to practice in the classroom, resulting in the publication of his book *Visible Learning for Teachers* (2012). It is through Hattie's work and my own study of visible learning that I have come to understand the assessment-capable learner and the attributes of such a learner. Assessment-capable learners (also discussed in depth in Chapter 1) are actively involved in their learning; they have a sound understanding of what they are learning and how they are progressing in their learning, and they are able to determine what they need to learn next.

The "fire" in me is roaring at this time because so many of the attributes that an assessment-capable learner exhibits can be nurtured and developed through the planning and implementation of performance tasks, whether they are used as learning experiences or as assessments. I just wish that I had known more about performance tasks and assessment-capable learners when I first started teaching.

Passion for Performance Tasks

My first experience with performance tasks—and I am using the term loosely—which I still remember clearly, was during my first year as a teacher at the Wellsville Middle School in the Southern Tier of New York. I was hired to teach seventh-grade social studies about three days before school started; I was to be a long-term sub (filling in for someone who was ill), responsible for teaching American history from exploration up to the Civil War. At times, I had students work in small learning groups, but what was most memorable was engaging them in tasks as their learning experience rather than as an assessment. A performance task can be the learning experience and not just an assessment of what students have learned—and that is the main premise of this book. Typically, when I used a performance task for learning content and processes, students also took a unit test at the end of the instructional period. A performance task, in my view, has students applying what they are learning as a means to learn (formative), or it can also be an application of what students have learned (summative), and the task is relevant because it makes the learning real.

Two performance tasks used during that year stand out in my mind 25-plus years later, and both were used as means for students to process their learning, not as assessments. The first performance task was the creation of a class "colonial newspaper" for which the students served as the reporters. Each student had to do some type of research and writing on colonial life and events to include in the newspaper, which we printed on 11-by-17-inch tabloid paper. As students were engaged in their learning through the performance task of being reporters for a colonial newspaper, the classroom was alive! The students were motivated to learn, and they were in control of their learning.

The second performance task I used as a learning experience was one focused on the American Revolution. Students worked in small groups and selected an event that led up to the American Revolution or was a key event during the Revolution. They then needed to research the event and present what they learned to the rest of the class; they could choose how they presented their information. One group knocked their presentation out of the park by reporting live from the Battle of Bunker Hill using the school's closed-circuit TV. This was about the time of the Iraq-Kuwait War, and that was the first time students had seen television reporting from the battlefield, with gunfire in the background. The students creatively modeled what they saw on real television by taking on the roles of television news reporters and reporting the news to the citizens (their classmates). Between the colonial newspaper performance task and the Battle of Bunker Hill presentation, I was able to further clarify how a performance task is defined.

These two performance tasks were not perfect by any means, but they led me to develop my own definition of a performance task, which is succinctly stated in Chapter 1. I did not have a model to follow to create or implement the tasks; I just used my best judgment based on what I had learned as an education student and first-year teacher. I often reflect on all I could have done to make these engaging learning experiences even more powerful, given what I know now. As the saying goes, hindsight is 20/20. These two performance tasks, in their infancy, sparked a "fire" in me about planning learning experiences for my classroom that would be relevant and motivating to students. I want to provide you with a process that can guide you through the development of performance tasks and accompanying scoring guides that will challenge and motivate students to want to learn and keep on learning even if it is difficult. By using performance tasks for learning and not just assessment, you can develop assessment-capable learners in your classroom.

Organization of This Book

Following this introduction, this book is organized into seven chapters:

- Chapter 1, "The Lasting Power of Performance Tasks," establishes a rationale for planning and creating performance tasks to use in your classroom.
- Chapter 2, "Building the Base: Begin With the End in Mind," focuses on standards, as they are at the center of every performance task. When it comes to any aspect of instructional planning and assessment, the standards are always the shining star.
- Chapter 3, "Building the Base: Learning Progressions," introduces the idea of learning progressions and makes connections to a few different practices with which you may already be familiar, in order to meld what you already know with something that may be new.
- Chapter 4, "Building the Base: Going SOLO!," discusses the SOLO (structure of the observed learning outcome) taxonomy and how it can support the creation of learning intentions and success criteria that build progressively from surface learning to deep learning.
- Chapter 5, "Performance Task Attributes," introduces the topic of how to create high-quality performance tasks that students will be motivated to complete and that will leave them wanting more. This chapter is not placed earlier in the book because before you plan a performance task, you should work through Chapters 2–4, which establish the base for the performance task.
- Chapter 6, "Scoring Guides, aka Rubrics," reviews scoring guides with the aim of providing some new insights that you can develop for your performance tasks.
- Chapter 7, "Implementation Considerations," is intended to help you with the implementation of performance tasks in your classroom, school, or district—or, for that matter, across a state. Why not think big?

As you progress through the chapters, you will encounter examples, mainly from core subject areas representing elementary and secondary grades, that will support your understanding of the key points of the concepts being discussed. Each chapter ends with a list of a few key takeaways, followed by a few questions for you to reflect upon. You will also have online access to a performance task planning template to complete a performance task as you read the book if you choose to do so. Consider allotting some additional time to reflect as well as to develop your own performance task as you are reading through the chapters. Chapter 2 is where you will start applying your learning by creating a performance task, if you choose to do so.

My hope is that as you read this book you will use the online planning template to create your own performance task and that you will try it out in your classroom. If you are an administrator, instructional coach, or other educational professional who does not have your own classroom, seek out a willing colleague who does have one to try your performance task with your support. When you implement performance tasks in your classroom, they will sound different and function differently than in other circumstances, so it is important to read the final chapter to ensure the success of your hard work in creating a performance task. It could potentially be a very important chapter for you no matter what your position.

I hope that once you engage your students in the completion of a performance task that you have created, you will feel like it is "the lighting of a fire" for both you and your students. Are you ready to be revved up about teaching and student learning through performance tasks?

1

The Lasting Power of Performance Tasks

Just like the fashion industry, education is notorious for recycling ideas. Bell-bottom pants may not be the latest rage, but boot-cut and wide-leg pants are close to the once-frenzied fashion trend of the 1970s. Educational initiatives and strategies often suffer the same fate as they arrive on the educational scene, each expected to be the "silver bullet" that will enhance student learning, improve student behavior, close the achievement gap, strengthen math fluency, or refine student writing. Yet educational initiatives begin to lose favor with teachers and administrators for various reasons, such as that they take too much time, or the results touted for them do not come to fruition, and thus the initiatives fade into the sunset, only to rise again years later with new names and/or a few adjustments.

That has been the fate of performance tasks, which essentially came on the education scene in the 1980s in the form of performance assessment. Performance assessment gained popularity in the 1980s and 1990s as the National Assessment of Educational Progress (NAEP) commenced pilot testing of performance assessments in mathematics and science in which students needed to demonstrate their learning and understanding, not just select responses. Several states dipped their toes into performance assessment, including Vermont, Kentucky, New York, and Maryland. Many states incorporated some form of performance assessment, even if it involved constructed responses, into their assessment systems (Darling-Hammond & Adamson, 2014). These states were the groundbreakers for performance assessment.

Performance assessment is not a stranger to educators abroad either—Finland, Singapore, Hong Kong, Australia, and England all utilize some form of performance assessment. The assessments in these countries challenge critical thinking skills and force students to apply their knowledge and skills to solve problems, conduct inquiries, and create products. Most of these countries "use a combination of centralized assessments that feature mostly open-ended and essay questions and school-based tasks which are factored into the final examination scores" (Darling-Hammond & Adamson, 2010, p. 14). Interestingly, England requires students seeking a general certificate of secondary education (GCSE) to be evaluated through a combination of open-ended test items and classroom performance tasks during and at the end of two years of study in a course. The New York State Regents Exams and the International Baccalaureate, as well as the assessment systems of Singapore, Hong Kong, and Australia, learned from England's GCSE assessment system as they developed their own systems (Darling-Hammond & Adamson, 2010).

However, with the passage of No Child Left Behind and testing moved from once a grade span to each grade level 3–8, the number of constructed-response questions diminished in many state assessments or disappeared altogether, replaced by multiple-choice questions. The increased use of multiple-choice questions in high-stakes assessments in turn changed classroom instruction, while at the same time accountability for student and school performance increased. Performance assessments of any format were fading away unless they were a part of a high-stakes accountability assessment.

As a result of the Common Core State Standards and the Next Generation Assessments created by the Smarter Balanced Assessment Consortium (SBAC) and the Partnership for Assessment of Readiness for College and Careers (PARCC)—the two organizations charged with developing assessment systems to measure student progress on the CCSS—performance assessments resurfaced as performance tasks. Just as some states opted out of the CCSS, they also opted out of the Next Generation Assessments, relying instead on their own state standards and assessments. Interestingly, performance tasks are now being welcomed with open arms as an alternative to selected-response items, especially in light of the need to prepare students to be college and career ready. Performance tasks serve as a powerful classroom practice that is beneficial for both students and teachers.

Performance tasks can serve as instructional learning experiences; as formative assessments for students, to adjust their learning tactics, and for teachers, to adjust their instructional practices and provide targeted feedback; as learning experiences for students, to help them develop the attributes of assessment-capable learners (a topic elaborated later in this chapter); and as a means for students to demonstrate what they have learned (summative performance tasks). Performance tasks have been on a roller-coaster ride over the past few decades, and they are currently experiencing a revival with the SBAC and PARCC Next Generation Assessments, which went online in 2015. However, change is in the air as a result of the Every Student Succeeds Act, with many states creating assessment plans to be ready for full implementation in the 2017–2018 school year. This could be the opportunity for educators to incorporate more performance tasks into classroom instruction as well as into assessment systems.

The Identity Crisis of Performance Tasks

Both performance tasks and performance assessments have been defined in numerous ways, and the definitions are often intertwined and have similar attributes. In some regards, it seems as if this is a nomenclature difference resulting from the rollout of the Next Generation Assessments and their incorporation of performance tasks in assessment models.

Mixed Messages

The multiple definitions of performance assessment and/or task can be problematic. In her book *Performance Assessment: Showing What Students Know and Can Do*, Susan Brookhart (2015) defines a performance assessment, which can be formative or summative in purpose, as an assessment "that (a) requires students to create a product or demonstrate a process, or both, and (b) uses observation and judgement based on clearly defined criteria to evaluate the qualities of student work" (p. 3). Larry Ainsworth (2015) defines performance tasks as "hands-on, active learning tasks that enable students to apply the concepts and skills they are learning by creating a product or performance that can be evaluated with a scoring guide" (p. 272). Jay McTighe (2015) defines a performance task as "any learning activity or assessment that asks students to perform or to demonstrate their knowledge, understanding and proficiency. Performance tasks yield a tangible product and/or performance that serves as evidence of student learning." Another term that is used in place of *performance assessment/task* is *authentic assessment* or *authentic task*. Giselle O. Martin-Kniep (2000) emphasizes the importance of students being engaged with "real-life problems, issues, or tasks for an audience who cares or has a stake in what students learn" (p. 26). Besides educational practitioners, the two assessment consortia SBAC and PARCC provide descriptions rather than definitions of performance tasks. SBAC states: "A Smarter Balanced performance task involves significant interaction of students with stimulus materials and/or engagement in a problem solution, ultimately leading to an exhibition of the students' application of knowledge and skills, often in writing or spoken language" (Measured Progress/ETS Collaborative, 2012, p. 1). In its online glossary, PARCC (n.d.) describes performance-based assessments (PBAs) as follows: "PBAs in math will focus on reasoning and modeling and include questions that require both short and extended responses. In ELA [English language arts]/literacy, the PBAs will focus on both reading comprehension and writing when analyzing texts."

The broad array of definitions for performance assessments crosses over into performance tasks. The bottom line is that it is difficult to define the difference between a performance assessment and a performance task. Linda Darling-Hammond and Frank Adamson recognize the dilemma of defining the meaning of performance assessment in *Beyond the Bubble Test: How Performance Assessments Support 21st Century Learning* (2014). They also incorporate the language of performance tasks as they explain how they are going to define the two terms for use in their book.

Given this book's focus on performance tasks, it seems appropriate at this point to ensure that you understand how I define performance tasks:

> A performance task is a **real-world product or performance** in which students **apply the concepts and/or skills** they are learning (formative) or have learned (summative) through a **motivating context**.

Let me break this down a bit to be sure you understand the meaning of the definition. *Real* here is not intended to equate to authentic. A "real-world product or performance" refers to students creating or performing what working people would do in their jobs and careers. A real-world product could be an accounting spreadsheet (accountant, business owner), a watercolor painting (artist, illustrator), or a short story (author). (A new volume of *The Best American Short Stories* is published every year, so don't think there are no authors writing short stories.) A real-world performance could be a debate (politician), an oral presentation (television reporter, marketing manager), a gymnastic routine (gymnast), or a cello performance (musician). The performance task needs to apply knowledge, skills, and understandings that students are learning or have learned. Students have to know something before they can apply it, but applying it can be in a formative situation and not a summative assessment.

Note that the definition specifies that performance tasks can be used as learning experiences in which formative feedback is provided or as summative assessments after students have learned the designated concepts and skills. The final component of the performance task is that there is a motivating context. Between the motivating context and the real-world product or performance, the learning becomes relevant to the students. So, if students taking the 11th-grade health elective course were to create a tasting menu for a farm-to-table restaurant, aiming to keep all entrées under 500 calories and appetizers under 300 calories, this would be considered a real-world performance. Restaurant owners, chefs, and caterers need to plan menus all the time and deal with special situations. Remember, in my definition, *real* is not intended to equate with authentic. If students in this 11th-grade health course were to attempt an authentic performance, they might work to revamp the school cafeteria's menu for the following year to meet the U.S. Department of Agriculture's standards for the National School Lunch and Breakfast Programs. The class might research the food likes and dislikes of students, learn about federal nutrition guidelines, and create menu options to present to the cafeteria manager. The main difference between real-world and authentic tasks is that a real-world task involves a product or performance that someone in an actual position or occupation would complete, but the situation is constructed by the teacher. An authentic task, in contrast, is a real-time product or performance that presents itself and is not purposefully constructed. Truly authentic tasks are few and far between because of the restrictions of what is currently occurring in a particular school or community.

Chapter 5 discusses in depth the attributes of a performance task, of which there are many beyond the concepts within the definition. Collectively, high-quality attributes make for the development of powerful performance tasks.

Figure 1.1 Performance Task Continuum

Basic Task   Real-World Task   Authentic Task

Student relevance, engagement, motivation

Performance Task Continuum

Given all of the varying definitions and descriptions of performance tasks/assessments, it seems that performance tasks fall along a continuum (see Figure 1.1). On one end of the continuum are completely authentic learning tasks. These are tasks in which a real-time situation in school or community is present, and the tasks become the vehicle for specific learning standards (as in the example above of the 11th-grade health class's menu options for the cafeteria). In the middle of the continuum are real-world performance tasks, in which situations are created that take into consideration actual jobs or occupations and products or performances that these positions would create (such as a caterer creating a menu for a private party with healthy, clean, and lean appetizer and entrée options). On the other end of the continuum are basic tasks requiring application of knowledge and skills, such as extended responses constructed from at least two sources of information. As performance tasks move along the continuum from basic tasks to authentic tasks, student relevance, engagement, and motivation increase. Single-word and simple single- or multiple-sentence responses do not constitute a performance task. At minimum, a performance task requires some type of application of knowledge and skills, not just knowing.

Reasons to Increase the Use of Performance Tasks

Common Core State Standards and Next Generation Assessments

As mentioned in the introduction, the Common Core State Standards are not only intended to prepare students for college and careers, but they are also "based on rigorous content and application of knowledge through higher-order thinking skills" (Common Core

State Standards Initiative, n.d.). The SBAC and PARCC's Next Generation Assessments are intended to measure the level of student understanding and application of the CCSS. Powerful performance tasks require the application of knowledge, skills, and understandings, and that is why the Next Generation Assessments include performance task sections—to measure students' ability to apply their learning to unique situations.

The original design of the Next Generation Assessments involved a combination of formative assessments to be used during the year with a summative assessment at the end of the year, and the current assessments fulfill that goal. However, whether states, districts, and schools utilize the formative assessments in conjunction with the summative may depend on how many assessments they are already requiring. This is an issue that Rick Stiggins (2006) and Linda Darling-Hammond (2014) are combatting. Darling-Hammond recognizes that the Next Generation Assessments are a step in the right direction as one means to measure higher-order thinking as demanded by the CCSS. However, high-stakes tests have limitations in their ability to demonstrate some kinds of student learning. Thus, such demonstration has to happen in the classroom, with the measurement of student understanding and application of research, writing, and oral skills through engagement in extensive research projects and oral and digital presentation of the findings. The Next Generation Assessments cannot be the sole means of determining student progress and learning.

Some schools are entering the arena of using a combination of assessments to measure student learning. Specifically, as Darling-Hammond (2014) writes:

> In addition to CCSS-aligned consortia exams, multiple measure could include:
>
> - Classroom-administered performance tasks (e.g., research papers, science investigations, mathematical solution, engineering designs, arts performances);
> - Portfolios of writing samples, art works, or other learning products;
> - Oral presentations and scored discussions; and
> - Teacher rating of student note-taking skills, collaboration skills, persistence with challenging tasks, and other evidence of learning skills.

These activities not only engage students in more intellectu-
ally challenging work that reflects 21st century skills, they
also serve as learning opportunities for teachers, when they
are involved in using the assessments and scoring them
together. (p. 11)

The 48 schools in the New York Performance Standards
Consortium have obtained permission to have students complete
performance tasks, or "projects," rather than take most Regents
Exams. The consortium has been in existence since the 1990s. For her
projects, one East Side Community High School senior researched
and wrote a paper on the Vietnam War and presented and defended
her paper in a 60-minute presentation to a faculty team, wrote an
analytical essay for English, conducted an experiment of her own
design for science, and completed an applied mathematics project.
Her performance on all of these projects determined whether she
would graduate from high school.

Research conducted on the New York consortium's schools
reveals that they have higher graduation rates and college enroll-
ment rates than other New York City schools, even though most
consortium students are considered low achieving. Specifically, the
graduation rate for East Side Community High School is 82% (four
years), compared to 68% on average across the city. However, there is
a downside to the data for East Side students: They do not perform
well on standardized tests such as the ACT, the SAT, and the one
Regents Exam they have to take. The defense of these data is that
such multiple-choice-dominated standardized tests represent a
"mismatch between the deep learning in the network's classrooms
and the kinds of knowledge that are tested on the SAT and Regents"
(Gewertz, 2015, p. 8). It seems that striking a balance with multiple
measures of assessment may be the best option, instead of going to
one extreme or the other.

The following comes from a fact sheet released by the White
House on December 2, 2015. This document summarizes and highlights some of the reform efforts in the new Every Student Succeeds
legislation, which at the time was headed to the Senate for approval.

A Smart and Balanced Approach to Testing: The bill maintains important statewide assessments to ensure that teachers
and parents can mark the progress and performance of their
children every year, from third to eighth grade and once in
high school. The bill encourages a smarter approach to testing

by moving away from a sole focus on standardized tests to drive decisions around the quality of schools, and by allowing for the use of multiple measures of student learning and progress, along with other indicators of student success to make school accountability decisions. It also includes provisions consistent with the Administration's principles around reducing the amount of classroom time spent on standardized testing, including support for state efforts to audit and streamline their current assessment systems. (para. 8)

In light of the Every Student Succeeds Act being signed into law, the Common Core State Standards and the Next Generation Assessments could be in jeopardy. Rigorous standards and yearly assessments in math and reading for grades 3–8 and once in high school are still required, but states now have control over what those will be, and they need to have their standards and assessments in place by 2017. Rick Stiggins and Linda Darling-Hammond might just succeed in promoting a resurgence of performance tasks as well as a focus on student learning versus student achievement.

Developing a Balanced and Thoughtful Assessment System

Stiggins and Darling-Hammond are the voices of reason in respect to the changes needed in national, state, and local assessment practices, and both have researched the topic for decades. In *Revolutionize Assessment* (2014), Stiggins pushes the envelope by stating, "Our testing practices are in crisis. They are currently doing as much harm as good for student learning" (p. 2). However, Darling-Hammond (2014) sees some glimmer of hope in the situation, as she expresses in her article "Testing to, and Beyond, the Common Core":

After more than a decade of test-driven, high-stakes accountability in the No Child Left Behind era, many educators and policymakers in the United States are looking to move toward a more thoughtful approach. Rather than maintaining a system that uses narrow measures of student achievement to sanction poorly performing schools, the push is now to implement next-generation learning goals that encourage higher-order thinking skills. (p. 10)

I am a proponent of performance tasks as instructional learning experiences, but such tasks have mainly been associated with summative assessment, as is the case with the Next Generation Assessments. Thus, it is important that states, districts, and schools develop balanced assessment systems in which different types of assessments serve different purposes for different users of the resulting information. The multiple measures cited above could all be used as instructional learning experiences as well as summative assessments. When a student is engaged in writing a research paper, this is not an on-demand task completed over a few class periods. The student is guided through a process and provided with feedback along the way. The final product serves as the summative assessment.

Prevailing Research

As mentioned in the introduction, research related to the field of education has become increasingly abundant. We now know what works best for student achievement growth thanks to the compilation of research by John Hattie, so why isn't every teacher in North America focusing on what works best? As a colleague once stated, "You wouldn't go to a doctor who does not stay current on the research in order to provide you with an accurate diagnosis or the best care." It would be a difficult challenge to find any educator, whether a classroom teacher, a director of special education, or a superintendent of schools, who says that he or she doesn't want to help kids learn. However, educators who are not staying current with educational research, and the implementation of that research, are not doing the most they can to help students learn to their greatest potential. John Hattie has written three books—*Visible Learning* (2009), *Visible Learning for Teachers* (2012), and, with Gregory Yates, *Visible Learning and the Science of How We Learn* (2014)—that have had profound impacts on teaching and learning.

Research Connections to Performance Tasks

In the development and implementation of performance tasks, a number of steps are based on Hattie's research as reported in *Visible Learning* (2009). For instance, the starting point to the development of a performance task—or any type of formative or summative assessment, for that matter—is "what" students need to learn. Teachers should not be the only ones who are privy to what students are learning during any given lesson or unit; the students should be cognizant of what they are learning as well, and know when they have attained the learning. Teacher clarity is an influence that Hattie describes in *Visible Learning*—it is about the teacher communicating to students the learning intention (what students are to learn) and its accompanying success criteria, to bring students into the learning process.

Effect Size

As noted above, a number of influences of Hattie's research are embedded in the planning and implementation of performance tasks. These include the concept of effect size, which is a means of measuring student achievement progress on a common scale. Hattie's determination to find out "What works best in education?" started his multiyear endeavor that resulted in the publication of *Visible Learning*, which synthesizes more than 800 meta-analyses concerning what influences student learning and to what extent. What is astonishing is that Hattie's research has been expanded to more than 1,000 meta-analyses and is still growing, while yielding the same results that were published in *Visible Learning* back in 2009.

Meta-analysis involves the combination of several research studies, in this case on educational influences. Hattie gathered hundreds of meta-analyses and analyzed various identified educational influences, such as "homework," to determine the impacts of those influences on student achievement. The statistical measure he used to compare all of these different influences is effect size. As Hattie (2012) explains, "An effect size is a useful method for comparing results on different measures (such as standardized, teacher-made tests, student work), or over time, or between groups, on a scale that allows comparisons independent of the original test scoring (for example, marked out of 10, or 100), across content, and over time" (p. 3).

What Hattie discovered in his original research was that if the bar for effectiveness is set at zero, about 95% of everything works. An additional finding was that the average effect size of the 800 original meta-analyses (plus the additional ones since the original research) was 0.40, and thus 0.40 became the "hinge-point" at which effectiveness of the influence is desired; this is considered to be about a year's worth of student growth (Hattie, 2012). Figure 1.2 provides an example of the "barometer of influences" developed by one of Hattie's colleagues to represent visually all the data he was compiling. It looks something like a protractor, with the arrow pointing to the effect size of a particular influence. In this case, the influence illustrated is teacher clarity, which has an effect size of 0.75. Note that effect sizes are broken into four quadrants: reverse effects (−0.20 to 0.00), developmental

Figure 1.2   Teacher Clarity Effect Size: "Barometer" Depiction

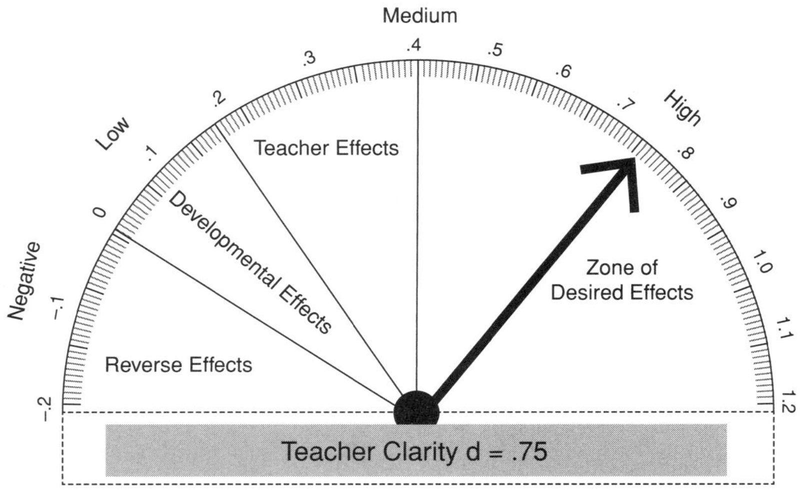

Source: Figure created by Josh McCarthy.

effects (approximately 0.10 to 0.18), teacher effects (0.19 to 0.40), and zone of desired effects (0.40 to 1.00+). Reverse effects are indicative of influences that result in student learning going backward rather than forward. Developmental effects are the effects students gain on their own based on maturity, and teacher effects are the typical influences that teachers have on student achievement. Finally, the zone of desired effects represents those influences that teachers should investigate further before making any final decisions (Hattie, 2012). As a teacher, what do you think your effect size is on student achievement?

Visible Learning is organized into contributions or educational influences from the student, home, school, teacher, curricula, and teaching approaches such as student motivation, home environment, retention, teacher–student relationships, reading, repeated readings, and reciprocal teaching. The book is a great resource, clarifying which influences work best to improve student achievement by placing all influences on the same scale—that is, effect size—but teachers should not use effect size alone to make decisions about influences; the text also offers important discussion on each influence and its effect size that further elaborates on different aspects of the research. For instance, homework has an effect size of 0.29. However, the summary of the research in *Visible Learning* explains that the effect size for homework at the elementary level is 0.15, while at the secondary level it is 0.64. It is essential that teachers not take effect size at face value, but dig deeper into the research, as it can reveal a tremendous amount of information (Hattie, 2009, 2012). Here are a few key points to keep in mind about effect size:

- The average effect size is 0.40, which equates to about a year of progress.
- The "hinge-point," or the point at which an influence is clearly affecting student learning, is an effect size of 0.40.
- An effect size of zero indicates no growth in student achievement.
- The zone of desired effects encompasses effect sizes of 0.40 and greater.
- A few influences have negative effect sizes, including summer vacation (−0.20), retention (−0.13), and mobility (−0.34).
- Teachers should read the research to discover the nuances within the effect sizes associated with particular influences.

Assessment-Capable Learners

Yes, in the United States the phrase *assessment-capable learners* is going to sound strange, except for those familiar with Hattie's work concerning visible learning. During my time as a remedial reading teacher, it was always more important to me that a student understood and could describe the meaning of a word than that he or she could just spew back a definition. This is the case with assessment-capable learners—that is, it is more useful to describe the characteristics of such learners than it is to give a definition. So, here goes—the characteristics of assessment-capable learners, as gleaned from the Visible Learning[plus] *Foundation Workbook* (n.d.-b) and *Building and Developing Visible Learners Workbook* (n.d.-a):

1. *Assessment-capable learners are aware of the learning intentions (what they are learning) and the success criteria (the criteria they need to demonstrate their learning and understanding of the learning intentions).* Students need to be aware of the learning intentions and success criteria so they can answer three key questions: "Where am I going?"; "How am I going?"; and "Where to next?" In many cases the performance task will be how students demonstrate the success criteria, so students will perform better if they know what they are learning and what success looks like.

2. *Assessment-capable learners use the success criteria and accompanying rubrics to self- and peer evaluate their progress in order to make adjustments if necessary.* Essentially, assessment-capable learners get, give, and act on feedback, and the scoring guides, or rubrics, that accompany performance tasks allow students to self- and peer evaluate progress and provide feedback. It is necessary to teach students how to give and get feedback from

peers as well as how to use the scoring guides as a means to self-evaluate.

3. *Assessment-capable learners use what James Popham (2008) would call "learning tactics" (p. 29) in order to progress in their learning as well as metacognitive strategies to monitor their learning tactics to ensure they are progressing.* It is necessary for students to plan their approach to the performance task and continually monitor and adjust as they progress through the task.

4. *Assessment-capable learners are actively involved in their learning and are eager to learn and progress.* They thrive on the challenge of learning and see mistakes as opportunities and not as failures. Performance tasks are intended to enable students to apply knowledge and skills, thus they need to be cognitively challenging. The self- and peer evaluations are opportunities for students to learn and go deeper with their learning.

Students are not receptacles into which we dump 13 years of education. They need to be active and engaged in their learning, and this has everything to do with the teachers they encounter in the classroom as well as the learning experiences those teachers plan and the instructional practices they utilize. If teachers use performance tasks as learning experiences and/or assessments and focus on developing assessment-capable learners, they will see achievement gaps close and students flourish in their classrooms.

The most exciting thing about assessment-capable learners is the fact that the development of such learners has had the highest effect size of any educational influence, 1.44, since 2009, only to be surpassed by collective self-efficacy (effect size 1.57) in the research released by Hattie in December 2015. Collective self-efficacy is the collective belief of the staff and students in a school that they can accomplish their common goals (Krownapple, 2015). Many different influences associated with performance tasks can help to develop assessment-capable learners, including collective self-efficacy.

Student Motivation and Relevance

Real-world performance tasks are powerful because they motivate students to learn; students see the relevance in learning and want to engage in the performance tasks. Motivation—defined by Merriam-Webster.com as "the act or process of giving someone a reason for doing something"—is an important aspect of the teaching and learning process. As teachers we have to give our students reasons to learn or to do things. When students are younger their intrinsic motivation to learn is high. Infants are determined to learn how to walk; we don't teach them how to put one foot in front of the other or maintain balance—children have an innate desire to learn to move. However, at times parents as well as teachers need to use extrinsic motivation. "If you eat all your peas, you can have a cookie for dessert"; "If you finish the math problems, you can have five extra minutes of recess"; or "If you turn in your homework tomorrow, you will receive five bonus points on your next test." It seems that as students age, their intrinsic motivation to learn diminishes. As Martin-Kniep (2011) observes: "Issues of engagement and motivation diminish greatly when students can appreciate the meaningfulness and relevance of what they are learning. This is what schooling should do for students. It should deepen their awareness of issues that matter, provide them with tools to transfer what they are learning into real-world applications, and inspire them to do good deeds" (p. 1). This is exactly what performance tasks can do for your classroom. Real-world and authentic performance tasks provide relevance for students, which results in motivation and engagement in learning.

New Opportunities

Performance tasks are on the rise and can become an integral part of classrooms, schools, and districts. The Common Core State Standards and the Next Generation Assessments brought performance tasks back to life after they had taken a backseat to the accountability measures of No Child Left Behind. Not only were the English language arts and math standards of the CCSS written as performance standards, the Next Generation Science Standards and the revised standards of the National Council for the Social Studies are now both written as performance standards. *Performance* means that the student creates or demonstrates a product or a performance in order to provide evidence of learning and progress. High-stakes assessments are administered once a year, and no matter the subject area, they are unable to measure many of the more involved standards. In addition to states being able to make decisions about rigorous standards, the Every Student Succeeds Act opens the door to the incorporation of multiple measures of assessment, including performance tasks, to determine students' levels of understanding and application of whatever standards are in place. Powerful real-world performance tasks can change a classroom, making it come alive. In such a vibrant environment, students are motivated and engaged in their learning. Both students and teachers are invigorated to learn!

Key Takeaways

- The early users of performance assessments forged the path for later revival of performance tasks.
- The CCSS and accompanying Next Generation Assessments have revived the use of performance tasks.
- Performance tasks and performance assessments have been defined in many ways, but the various definitions encompass many common characteristics.
- A performance task is defined in this book as a real-world product or performance in which students apply the concepts and/or skills they are learning (formative) or have learned (summative) through a motivating context.
- Real-world performance tasks are powerful tasks that provide relevance and motivation to learners.
- Performance tasks fall along a continuum that corresponds with student relevance, engagement, and motivation.

Figure 1.1   Performance Task Continuum

- The development and implementation of performance tasks supports the development of assessment-capable learners, which has an effect size of 1.44. The average effect size is 0.40.
- The Every Student Succeeds Act can open doors for an increase in the use of performance tasks.
- There is a need for balanced assessment systems that utilize multiple measures, including in-class performance tasks, instead of relying on one high-stakes assessment.

Reflection Questions

1. What is the extent of the use of performance tasks, along the continuum described in this chapter, in your classroom, school, or district?

2. Why are you interested in the use of performance tasks for instruction and assessment?

3. What roadblocks are currently in place preventing you from incorporating more performance tasks? What can you do to overcome the roadblocks?

4. What resonated with you the most in this chapter and why?

2

Building the Base

Begin With the End in Mind

Developing the Performance Task Base

The introduction and Chapter 1 have set the stage for the development of a performance task. When it comes to creating a performance task, you have to start by developing the base. All instructional learning experiences and all assessments, whether they are formative or summative, are generated from the base. If the base is weak, both the learning experiences and the assessments will be weak.

There are a few steps to developing the base, some you may be familiar with and others that may be new to you. The base steps consist of identifying standards for a unit of instruction, creating learning progressions, and determining the learning intentions/success criteria utilizing the SOLO (structure of the observed learning outcome) taxonomy. Once the base has been developed, it is time to start thinking about instruction and assessment. This is where performance tasks come into play. This chapter focuses on standards for a reason: Standards are the starting point for the development of the performance task. Chapters 3 and 4 complete the building of the base for the performance task, but all steps focus on the identified standards of the unit of instruction. The standards are the cornerstone to the base.

Establishing a Clear Focus for Learning

As with most processes, in developing a performance task you need to begin with the end in mind. Where are you going? If you don't know where you're going, it can be rather difficult to get anywhere. A few years back, my husband and I moved our household from Central Florida to Walla Walla, Washington. We knew, very clearly, that Walla Walla was our final destination. It did not matter that in mid-May we had to spend the night in Colby, Kansas, because of a late-winter storm that closed Colorado and Wyoming highways, and backtrack to a southern route through the Texas Panhandle. Our destination remained the same—Walla Walla, Washington.

In developing a performance task, you need to have a laserlike focus on your destination—in this case, the destination is what students need to learn. This is the nonnegotiable of performance tasks. Other learning is definitely going to take place in the process, and that is natural and should be welcomed and encouraged. The point is, what students need to learn remains steadfast, no matter what challenges you and the students encounter along the way. If a roadblock appears, you may need to try a different learning route, but your aim is to arrive at the same destination.

In regard to a performance task, the standards within a unit of instruction are ultimately what students need to learn. They are the final destination and will remain the destination from planning through instruction and then through assessment. You might know these standards well, but you are going to get to know them even better, as they are the linchpin of the base for the performance task. You will get to know your standards so well while building the base, it will be as if they moved into your spare bedroom and are making themselves at home in your family room.

The Standards

As discussed in Chapter 1, the Every Student Succeeds Act requires U.S. states to establish rigorous standards for all students, but states are not required to retain the Common Core State Standards. Thus, the standards saga continues. In the scheme of performance tasks, however, it does not matter what standards you are using as long as standards are at the heart of each performance task. Standards for your subject area should be the basis of all your instructional planning, whether you are planning instructional learning experiences or assessments. The standards determine the nonnegotiable end destination—that is, what students ultimately need to learn.

It is not good practice to come up with an idea for a performance task before you know what standards will be the focus of the unit of instruction. The standards are the focus of the learning, and the performance or product is the vehicle for learning or assessing. If you have an idea for a performance task first, you are then forced to "fit" standards into the unit rather than the standards being in the driver's seat.

The Common Core State Standards

At the time I began writing this book, the Common Core State Standards were being implemented in 42 states, the District of Columbia, four U.S. territories, and the Department of Defense Education Activity instructional program. For the time being, the CCSS are the predominant standards, at least until states establish their action plans in compliance with the Every Student Succeeds Act. The CCSS were finalized in 2010, and states began the process of adopting the standards, as many of them were vying for the Race to the Top funds that were available. Although ESSA does not require states to use the CCSS, there is really no reason they should dismiss the standards, which are rigorous (as discussed in Chapter 1). The uproar around the CCSS is more about how states, districts, and schools have gone about implementation of the standards than about the standards themselves.

The two CCSS documents (one for mathematics, here referred to as the Math CCSS, and one for English language arts and literacy in history/social studies, science, and technical subjects, referred to here as the ELA CCSS) are organized differently, but both outline expectations for what students should know and be able to do at each grade level. The ELA CCSS document specifies that the standards are not all-inclusive of what students need to know and be able to do; rather, the standards encourage the formation of a "well-developed, content-rich curriculum" that incorporates grade-level expectations (Common Core State Standards Initiative, 2010a, p. 6). The introduction to the Math CCSS document states, "These Standards do not dictate curriculum or teaching methods" (Common Core State Standards Initiative, 2010b, p. 5). Both documents outline the expectations for what students should learn at each grade level, but these expectations are not the curriculum. Curriculum needs to be developed from the standards in each of the CCSS documents.

Other Content-Area Standards

English language arts and mathematics are not the only content areas in town. Standards have been established for other content areas as well, delineating student expectations either by grade level or by grade-level bands, such as grades 3–5, depending on the subject area. The Next Generation Science Standards have followed the lead of the CCSS, adopting a "common" set of standards and updating the science standards that were in place. We all know that in recent decades the field of science has exploded and numerous scientific advances have been made; thus, science standards need to reflect new knowledge and understandings. The Next Generation Science Standards, which are intended to make students college ready in the area of science, were finalized and published online in April 2013. At the time of this writing, they have been adopted by only a handful of states. In many cases, however, districts within states that have not adopted the standards are adopting them on their own (Heitin, 2015). The Next Generation Science Standards have made it a bit easier for science teachers to integrate the ELA CCSS and the Math CCSS by providing recommendations for ELA connections and math connections for each science standard. For those teaching science, the Next Generation Science Standards offer a great opportunity to create performance tasks that integrate subject-area standards. The National Council for the Social Studies recently revised its standards as well, and some states, including Illinois, have used the council's College, Career, and Civic Life (C3) Framework as the guiding focus for the revision of their social studies standards.

Additionally, the core subject areas are not the only ones with standards. A variety of organizations have created standards for other content areas, such as the American Council on the Teaching of Foreign Languages; its National Standards for Learning Languages align with the ELA CCSS. SHAPE America (the Society of Health and Physical Educators) has developed the National Physical Education Standards. If no national organization has developed standards for your particular subject area, your state has most certainly developed standards for that area. In any content area, states can either adopt standards that were created by a national educational organization or write standards for themselves.

Final Thoughts on Standards

In all cases, the standards represent what students need to learn, and they are the final destination. Depending on how the standards are written, they may state only what students need to know and be able to do, or they may also include what students need to understand, which takes the learning a step further. The key thing to remember about all standards, however, is that even though they represent the expectations of what students are to learn, they are *not* the curriculum. The standards are the foundation for developing a curriculum, and no matter what state, district, or school you work in, or what subject area you teach, standards are available. Once you have your standards, you need to understand the meaning of those standards, and, depending on how many standards are present in your subject area, you may need to determine which standards will be a primary focus during instruction. Not all standards are created equal.

Curriculum Development

Units of Instruction

Curriculum is generally organized around the unit of instruction. The ELA CCSS document encourages teachers to develop units of instruction by grouping the standards together rather than teaching and assessing them individually:

> While the Standards delineate specific expectations in reading, writing, speaking, listening, and language, each standard need not be a separate focus for instruction and assessment. Often, several standards can be addressed by a single rich task. (Common Core State Standards Initiative, 2010a, p. 5)

What is interesting about this statement is that although it notes that "several standards can be addressed by a single rich task," it does not specify whether that rich task is part of the instruction or part of an assessment. That is the beauty of performance tasks, as they can be used either way.

Standards are the foundation of curriculum development, and a unit of instruction is "a series of specific lessons, learning experiences, and related assessments" organized around selected standards (Ainsworth, 2010, p. 61). The units of instruction create the curriculum for a course or subject. There are four major types of units of instruction: topical, skills-based, thematic, and interdisciplinary. The topical unit of study is probably the most common type. Topical units address particular topics; they might have names like

The Industrial Revolution, The Planets, The Short Story, or Fractions. Skills-based units center on the application of skills, such as map reading, measuring liquid amounts, identifying the author's point of view, or graphing. Thematic units often cross disciplines or "emphasize connections" within a discipline. For example, a thematic unit in social studies might be named Revolution, one in science might be Life Cycles, one in English might be Change, and one in math might be Patterns (Ainsworth, 2010). Finally, interdisciplinary units of study involve standards from two or more content areas (Glass, 2013). Almost any topical unit of study could become interdisciplinary with the addition of a reading, writing, or speaking standard from the ELA CCSS. Math and science are good partners for interdisciplinary units. Organizing curriculum around interdisciplinary units is beneficial for students because it reinforces the idea that life is not broken up into math or science or English time; rather, the real world integrates what they have learned in all subject areas.

Teacher Collaborative Planning

Teaching is a complicated process that involves a lot of ongoing decision making aimed at student learning. When done well, it provides motivating rewards for both students and teachers. Students become invested and engaged in learning, and teachers are driven to continue to plan learning experiences that challenge, motivate, and stretch student learning. When it comes to methods of planning instruction, "the most powerful is when teachers work together to develop plans, develop common understandings of what is worth teaching, collaborate on understanding their beliefs of challenge and progress, and work together to evaluate the impact of their planning on student outcomes" (Hattie, 2012, p. 37). Two teachers at W. Reily Brown Elementary School in Delaware, Michelle Caulk and Emily Peterson, created a performance task using the template provided in this book, working collaboratively in the planning process. When they later shared their reflections on this process, both teachers mentioned collaboration. Michelle wrote: "It was enlightening to connect with colleagues, to share thoughts, and provide support. We were able to draw the knowledge and skills of one another to plan and design an effective performance task. Using Ms. Shiel's performance task template, we were able to use common language and remain focused on our common goal." You and your teaching colleagues should capitalize on the power of collective minds working together and start planning your units of instruction together, just as Michelle Caulk and Emily Peterson did in Delaware.

A Look at Curriculum

As a result of the adoption and implementation of the CCSS in so many states, curriculum development around the CCSS has become very prevalent. The curricular documents available to you in your subject area(s) are likely to vary depending on the state, district, or school in which you teach. No matter where you are, however, you can access the websites of all state departments of education as well as many school districts and individual schools. Extensive documents are available online, including curricular documents. For example, you can access the New York State Department of Education, which has developed comprehensive curricular documents using the ELA CCSS and Math CCSS for all teachers to implement. Or you can go to the website of the Kentucky Department of Education and learn about the guidance the state provides to districts and schools on developing curriculum. Kentucky does not dictate the curricula for its districts; rather, it provides supporting documents to assist districts in developing their own curricula. These documents include a deconstruction of each of the standards in the ELA CCSS and the Math CCSS. As noted above, the Illinois Department of Education has followed the C3 Framework created by the National Council for the Social Studies in revising its social studies curriculum (Illinois Social Science Standards Revision Task Force, 2015). When it comes to implementation of the CCSS, since the standards were established each state has taken its own approach, with some being very directive to their districts and others providing only support and guidance as districts took on the endeavor of implementation.

In the states that have left curriculum development up to the individual districts, there is yet another level of variety. Some districts have been very directive, creating and providing teachers with curricular documents to follow. For instance, one elementary curricular document I have seen provides a week-by-week outline of the standards to be taught in the areas of English language arts, social studies, and science. The document only provides the standards—it is not organized into units of instruction, so teachers need to decide how to organize the standards for instruction (this is an instance where teacher collaborative planning would come in handy). In a different district I viewed several middle school social studies curriculum maps, all organized differently. One of these initially maps out the units for the year and includes both content standards and CCSS for Literacy in History/ Social Studies, Science, and Technical Subjects and a writing requirement with each unit. As you move through the document, each unit is further outlined. Within the unit, the full text of all the standards (content, CCSS) is stated, along with suggestions for resources and possible activities to address each of the standards. In some cases, multiple standards are shown for an activity. Another curriculum map I have viewed has five columns labeled "Content" (standards), "Knowledge," "Skills," "Assessment/Resources," and "Time." It is interesting that assessment and resources are in one column together.

Curriculum development is a challenging process, and curricular documents come in all formats, some with a wide variety of information and others with only limited information. In some cases there are no curricular documents at all; instead, textbooks, such as *The American Nation* or *Journeys,* or computer programs, such as Read 180 or Time4Learning Math, are considered the curriculum, when in fact they are just resources to use within a curriculum.

Just as there were concerns about states having different educational standards and the quality of those standards (concerns that became the driving force behind the development of the Common Core State Standards), questions have arisen about the curricula that have been and are being developed by states, districts, or schools for the CCSS as well as all other standards. Some curricula are written and organized well, but some are questionable. Not all curricular documents are created equal. In the words of Lois Lanning (2013):

> The Common Core State Standards . . . target the performances students are expected to demonstrate. If we do not design curriculum that provides teachers with a clear, unambiguous picture of *how to teach to understanding,* the Common Core State Standards will become yet another initiative that fails to impact student learning or the state of education in our country. (p. 8)

This statement brings up two important points. First, the CCSS and most other subject-area standards are written in broad terms and do not specify everything students need to know or be able to do, or, more important, what they need to understand about the standards they are learning. Second, the fact is that students are expected to "perform" to demonstrate their learning of the standards, and each standard has embedded within it many things that students need to learn (knowledge, skills, and understandings) and thus demonstrate.

The CCSS, the Next Generation Science Standards, and the standards of the National Council for the Social Studies have a lot of depth within each standard, but they also provide global overviews of what students should know, understand, and be able to do. Once the standards are placed in units of instruction, they need to be broken down into the nuts and bolts of what students need to learn in order to demonstrate understanding and application of the standards. These are performance standards, so the intention is that students should be able to demonstrate the standards in some manner.

Planning Instruction and Assessment

No matter whether you are planning instruction or assessment, you have to build a base. The first step in building the base is a two-part process. First, you need to identify a unit of instruction, which is the building block for your curriculum. Next, you must select the standards to be taught and assessed in the unit of instruction. The standards will mainly be from the content area you teach, but they could also include other curricular areas—an approach that can be beneficial. For instance, if you teach social studies, oral and written communication is also important, and you should work to incorporate the CCSS for Literacy in History/Social Studies in your unit of study.

As for the number of standards to include, there is no hard-and-fast rule. Just as an example, on the New York State Education Department's EngageNY website (www.engageny.org), I found an 11th-grade English unit that included 11 grade-level standards from the areas of reading, writing, speaking and listening, and language. In *Rigorous Curriculum Design* (2010), Larry Ainsworth recommends including three to four priority standards in a unit. Priority standards are a selected subset of the full content-area standards that are deemed to be of greater importance than others. In this approach, standards are not eliminated; rather, they are prioritized for learning. Each unit of instruction should have a small, cohesive group of standards that are the primary focus of learning for the unit—these are the priority standards. A few other standards may be included as well, but they should be viewed as having secondary importance for that particular unit of study.

The standards that are selected for a unit of study are end-of-year expectations, so if in a particular unit you are focusing only on a certain aspect of a standard, or a few aspects, you should somehow indicate what portion of the standard is not being addressed in the unit and will be left to be included in another unit. For instance, the grade 3 reading standard shown in Appendix 2 includes several genres, but for this particular unit the focus is solely on stories. Thus, I indicated that I was focusing on the stories in this unit by striking out the other types of genres as well as "lesson" and "moral," which are associated with the other genres mentioned. Let's take a deeper look at one portion of a social studies standard:

CE.2 The student will apply social science skills to understand the foundations of American constitutional government by
   a) explaining the fundamental principles of consent of the governed, limited government, rule of law, democracy, and representative government.

The standard is not all-inclusive of what students need to know, understand, and be able to do; rather, it is the starting point to making these determinations. H. Lynn Erickson (2007) has observed that curriculum has traditionally been "two-dimensional," focusing only on what students need to know and be able to do—conceptual understanding has been the missing link. It is interesting to note that the ELA CCSS document states that the standards delineate what students should know and be able to do; it makes no mention of what they need to understand. On the other hand, the Math CCSS document indicates that the standards focus on conceptual understanding and that they delineate what students should understand and be able to do in mathematics (Common Core State Standards Initiative, 2010a, 2010b). John Hattie also stresses the need to challenge students so that they move beyond surface learning to deep learning and conceptual understanding. It is clear that no matter what the standards are, it is necessary to stretch students' learning in this way. Chapter 4 discusses these concepts in depth.

Finally, as James Popham (2008) espouses, once you know your curricular target, you need to develop the possible learning progression that will help students move toward the curricular goal. Basically, you need to teach students the knowledge and skills necessary to reach the curricular goal, which ends up being the primary standard.

Once you have selected the standards for a unit of instruction, you must break down the standards to determine what students really need to know, do, and understand and the proposed order of their learning. This is the focus of the next chapter, which presents some of the best thinking of educational professionals so that you can merge your present knowledge with new knowledge in a way that works for you.

Building the Base Step 1: Identify a Unit of Study and Select Standards

When it comes to creating a performance task, as noted above, you start with the building of the base, and standards are housed in units of instruction. As the first step in building the base, you need to perform two basic tasks:

1. *Identify a unit of instruction in your curriculum.* It can be in any subject area: mathematics, music, instructional technology, science, English language arts, or another area. Depending on your state, district, or school, you may already have curriculum organized around units of instruction. If not, you can select for yourself a topical, thematic, skills-based, or interdisciplinary unit that you intend to start in two or three weeks. Consider an interdisciplinary unit, with standards from more than one content area.

2. *Select the standards for the unit of instruction.* It is recommended that you select three to five primary standards that will be the focus of the learning. You may know these as priority or power standards. You may also select a couple of secondary standards that will serve a supporting role in the unit of study. If you are an English teacher and have identified an interdisciplinary unit of study, don't hesitate to select social studies or science content standards as secondary standards; if you are a science or social studies teacher, consider incorporating the CCSS for Literacy in History/Social Studies, Science, and Technical Subjects.

Figure 2.1, 2.2, and 2.3 provide examples of units of study listing the primary and secondary standards that are the focus of learning.

Figure 2.1   Grade 3 Unit, Mathematics, Primary and Secondary Standards

---

Grade 3—Mathematics

Unit: Tick Tock, It Never Stops!

Primary Standards

Use place value understanding and properties of operations to perform multi-digit arithmetic.

3.NBT.2 Fluently add and subtract within 1,000 using strategies and algorithms based on place value, properties of operations, and/or the relationship between addition and subtraction.

Solve problems involving measurement and estimation of intervals of time, liquid volumes, and masses of objects.

3.MD.1 Tell and write time to the nearest minute and measure time intervals in minutes. Solve word problems involving addition and subtraction of time intervals in minutes, e.g., by representing the problem on a number line diagram.

Secondary Standards

3.W.2 Write informative/explanatory texts to examine a topic and convey ideas and information clearly.

    a.   Introduce a topic and group-related information together; include illustrations when useful to aiding comprehension.

    b.   Develop the topic with facts, definitions, and details.

Figure 2.2   Grade 8 Unit, English Language Arts, Primary and Secondary Standards

---

Grade 8—English Language Arts

Unit: Narrative Analysis and Opinion Writing

Primary Standards

RL.8.2 Determine a theme or central idea of a text and analyze its development over the course of the text, including its relationship to the characters, setting, and plot; provide an objective summary of the text.

RL.8.3 Analyze how particular lines of dialogue or incidents in a story or drama propel the action, reveal aspects of a character, or provoke a decision.

W.8.1 Write arguments to support claims with clear reasons and relevant evidence.

    a.   Introduce claim(s), acknowledge and distinguish the claim(s) from alternate or opposing claims, and organize the reasons and evidence logically.

    b.   Support claim(s) with logical reasoning and relevant evidence, using accurate, credible sources and demonstrating an understanding of the topic or text.

c. Use words, phrases, and clauses to create cohesion and clarify the relationships among claim(s), counterclaims, reasons, and evidence.

d. Establish and maintain a formal style.

e. Provide a concluding statement or section that follows from and supports the argument presented.

Secondary Standards

RL.8.1 Cite the textual evidence that most strongly supports an analysis of what the text says explicitly as well as inferences drawn from the text.

L.8.2 Demonstrate command of the conventions of standard English capitalization, punctuation, and spelling when writing.

a. Use punctuation (comma, ellipsis, dash) to indicate a pause or break.

b. Use an ellipsis to indicate an omission.

c. Spell correctly.

Figure 2.3 High School Unit, Virginia and U.S. History, Primary and Secondary Standards

High School—History

Unit: Foundations of American Government

Primary Standards

CE.2 The student will apply social science skills to understand the foundations of American constitutional government by

a. explaining the fundamental principles of consent of the governed, limited government, rule of law, democracy, and representative government;

b. examining and evaluating the impact of the Magna Carta, charters of the Virginia Company of London, the Virginia Declaration of Rights, the Declaration of Independence, the Articles of Confederation, and the Virginia Statute for Religious Freedom on the Constitution of Virginia and the Constitution of the United States, including the Bill of Rights;

c. describing the purposes for the Constitution of the United States as stated in its Preamble; and

d. describing the procedures for amending the Constitution of Virginia and the Constitution of the United States.

CE.6 The student will apply social science skills to understand the American constitutional government at the national level by

a. explaining the principle of separation of powers and the operation of checks and balances.

(Continued)

Figure 2.3 (Continued)

Secondary Standards

R.HS.11.12.2 Determine the central ideas or information of a primary or secondary source; provide an accurate summary that makes clear the relationships among the key details and ideas.

W.HS.11.12.2 Write informative/explanatory texts, including the narration of historical events, scientific procedures/experiments, or technical processes.

Follow Along: Creating a Performance Task

Starting with this chapter and ending with Chapter 6, you will have the opportunity to create your own performance task as you follow along with each chapter. Chapters 2, 3, and 4 develop the base for the performance task. Chapter 5 focuses on designing the performance task itself, and Chapter 6 supports the development of scoring guides for the performance task.

At this time, if you are ready to take the plunge and create a performance task for a unit, follow the guidelines below. You can access a planning template on this book's page at the Corwin website (http://www.corwin.com/books/Book249034). Use the examples provided in Figures 2.1–2.3 to guide the development of your performance task. On the performance task template:

1. Fill in the general information of teacher/team, grade level/ subject area, and unit type and title.

2. Identify three to five primary standards that are the focus of the unit, and place the full text of the standards in the template in Step 1. Then select one or two secondary standards that support the primary standards and place the full text of those standards in the template following the primary standards.

Key Takeaways

- The base is the foundation for the performance task.
- The standards remain the central focus throughout the development of the performance task. All parts of the base lead back to the standards.
- Curriculum documents vary greatly at all levels (school, district, state) and even within schools, districts, and states.

- Two heads are better than one. Plan collaboratively with colleagues for deeper understanding of the standards and enhanced performance tasks.
- Units of study are the simplest way to organize curriculum.
- The performance task base starts with the standards and is followed by the development of learning progressions and then SOLO learning intentions and success criteria.
- Some standards are more important than others to learn; thus, standards should be prioritized, with some designated as primary and others as secondary.

Reflection Questions

1. What is the status of curricular documents in your classroom, grade or department, school, or district?

2. Based on their status, which curricular documents do you think will be helpful in performance task development? Are there any that could hinder performance task development?

3. Are there any curricular documents that you would be willing to revise as part of your performance task learning?

4. Are you familiar with the concepts of priority and supporting standards? How are these similar to the primary and secondary standards discussed in this chapter?

5. What resonated with you the most in this chapter and why?

3

Building the Base

Learning Progressions

Once the cornerstone of the base—consisting of the primary and secondary standards for a unit of instruction—is in place, you can proceed with the construction of the base. The standards typically represent the grade-level, or grade-span, year-end outcomes, depending on your subject area. They are what you want students to know and be able to do by the end of the year, not necessarily by the end of a given unit. For many of the standards, in particular the primary standards, students need multiple exposures in a variety of contexts in order to gain deep understanding and be able to apply what they've learned by the end of the school year.

Because the standards represent the desired end result for the year, you must think of the stepping-stones that students will need to make progress during the year, so that by year's end they will be able to demonstrate their understanding and application of the standard for their grade level. As Margaret Heritage (2010) notes, "Learning involves progression" (p. 38). Students must progress from their present state of understanding to the end goal. Merriam-Webster.com defines the verb *progress* as "to improve or develop over a period of time," and that is the intent of the standards, for students to learn and apply them over the school year. Developing learning progressions for the primary standards you have identified is the next phase in building the base for your performance task. However, please note that the base is necessary for planning all instruction and assessment, of which a performance task could be a part. Let's take a closer look at what learning progressions are and why they are important in the planning process and in the development of performance tasks.

Learning Progressions: Definitions and Descriptions

Learning progressions have been defined and described in a number of different ways, and other terms have been used that have the same meaning; however, in the United States the term *learning progression* has prevailed over *task analysis, learning continuum,* and *progress map* (which remains the predominant term in Australia). Additionally, it seems that certain fields of study—such as mathematics, science, and English language arts—are at the forefront in the use of learning progressions, with mathematics leading the pack and science coming on strong as a result of the Next Generation Science Standards (Achieve, 2015).

In *Transformative Assessment,* W. James Popham (2008) defines a learning progression as "a sequenced set of subskills and bodies of enabling knowledge that, it is believed, students must master en route to mastering a more remote curricular aim. In other words, it is composed of the step-by-step building blocks students are presumed to need in order to successfully attain a more distant, designated instructional outcome" (p. 24). Heritage (2010) describes learning progressions as "pathways along which students are expected to progress" (p. 38). Several other researchers have provided definitions as well, including Masters and Forster (1996), who state that a learning progression is "a description of skills, understanding and knowledge in the sequence in which they typically develop: a picture of what it means to 'improve' in an area of learning" (p. 1). Another commonly cited definition of learning progressions is that they are "descriptions of successively more sophisticated ways of thinking about an idea that follow one another as students learn: they lay out in words and examples what it means to move toward more expert understanding" (National Research Council, 2006, p. 3). Finally, Karin Hess (2008), who has done extensive work with learning progressions, offers the following four "guiding principles of learning progressions," or LPs:

- "LPs are developed (and refined) using available research."
- "LPs have clear binding threads that articulate the essential core concepts and processes" of a discipline (sometimes called the "big ideas" of a discipline).

- "LPs articulate movement toward increased understanding" (meaning deeper, broader, more sophisticated understanding).
- "LPs go hand-in-hand with well-designed/aligned assessments." (p. 3)

There is a lot of information to process on learning progressions, especially given the number of different perspectives on them among educational practitioners. The education reform organization Achieve gathered together educational practitioners and district policy leaders to discuss the growing research on learning progressions and discovered that the field has not yet established a consistent language or consistent definitions of terms, as demonstrated by the series of definitions quoted above. For the sake of their discussions and presentation of their findings (in *The Role of Learning Progressions in Competency-Based Pathways*, 2015), the practitioners and district policy leaders gathered by Achieve agreed that learning progressions "map out commonly travelled paths that students take" (p. 2). Take note of the phrase "commonly travelled," as this is an important aspect of learning progressions. Basically, the definitions quoted above point out some similar and some different aspects about learning progressions. In an attempt to meld these all together in a comprehensive manner, I came up with the following definition:

> Learning progressions target a goal in a subject area by delineating the key stepping-stones (knowledge and skills) students need to learn to achieve the goal; they are placed in a well-informed visual or verbal order.

One of the tasks that the Achieve work group was charged with accomplishing was to identify some common areas of agreement about learning progressions. The participants found four basic points of agreement. First, they noted that "learning progressions describe conceptual milestones in student learning and are sometimes referred to as the 'messy middle' between a student's present understanding and where educators need the student to end up" (Achieve, 2015, p. 3). This point is rather interesting in light of the implementation of the CCSS. The second point of agreement is that learning progressions should be based on empirical evidence gathered by researchers and practitioners observing student learning pathways and used to make adjustments to the learning progressions. The third point of agreement, which makes perfect sense, is that there is no perfect learning progression. Students are not all going to take the same pathway to get to the same outcome. Just look at the language in Heritage's, Popham's, and Achieve's definitions. They use words and phrases such as "expected" pathways, "presumed to be," and "commonly travelled paths." No learning progression is perfect! Learning progressions must be continually refined based on observations of student pathways, misconceptions, and research on learning. This third point of agreement is closely related to the first, as students come with different experiences, knowledge, and skills in relation to the curricular goal. Thus, students will be starting in different places, and some will have further to go than others. Chapter 7 provides a discussion of prior knowledge, as it has a tremendous impact on the planning and instructional process. Another reason there is no perfect learning progression is that students bring different levels of motivation to learn, as well as different learning strengths and challenges. The final point of agreement among the practitioners and researchers is that there is a balance between content and skills in student learning (Achieve, 2015). That is, learning progressions encompass both what students need to know (content and concepts) and what students are to do with the knowledge. These four points of agreement basically describe the characteristics of learning progressions. As the research on learning progressions continues to grow, practitioners and district policy leaders may find that they agree on additional characteristics.

Importance of Learning Progressions

Learning progressions are moving more and more into the forefront of education as information about how students learn and how the brain functions is becoming increasingly available. Learning progressions can potentially play a critical role in enhancing both instruction and assessment, as well as in engaging students in their learning progress (Achieve, 2015). Learning progressions can help students dig deeper into the primary standards, and once a learning progression is established, it can provide you with guidance on the appropriate time to assess students formatively before progressing with instruction.

Targeting Learning

As you develop a learning progression for a standard, you are clearly defining what students need to learn. It is as if you are focusing a microscope—as you adjust the lens, the standard becomes clearer and clearer. You are targeting potential student stepping-stones for learning. The standards that have been selected for a unit of instruction do not necessarily delineate everything that students need to learn; thus, it is up to teachers and teacher teams to determine what students need to learn by identifying the bigger stepping-stones, not the wobbly smaller ones, along the way to attaining the year-end goal.

This CCSS second-grade math standard (measurement and data) on time provides an example: "2.MD.7: Tell and write time from analog and digital clocks to the nearest five minutes, using a.m. and p.m." In first grade, students were introduced to telling and writing time to the half hour and hour on analog and digital clocks, but they were not introduced to the concept of a.m. and p.m. So the question becomes, What is it that students need to learn in order to be able to tell time on both styles of clocks and write time in the correct format using a.m. and p.m.? What is the knowledge, and what are the skills that accompany the knowledge? I came up with the following list, taking into consideration the first-grade standard. (Keep in mind that this is *not* a learning progression, just an exercise to point out the fact that in the process of developing a learning progression, student learning becomes clarified and targeted for both the teacher and the student.)

2.MD.7 Tell and write time from analog and digital clocks to the nearest five minutes, using a.m. and p.m.

- Define the hours of a.m. and p.m.
- Explain the significance of noon.
- Count intervals of 5 to 60.
- State number of hours in a day.
- Write time in correct format.
- Compare and contrast analog clocks to digital clocks.
- State time to the three-quarters hour, quarter hour, every 10 minutes.
- Identify time at which a new day starts.
- Round to the nearest 5 minutes.

This list represents the "subskills and enabling knowledge" discussed by Popham (2008). Popham's definition and process are emphasized in this chapter because they are the ones that resonate with me the most when it comes to applicability. Instruction can be enhanced just by this simple exercise of thinking backward. In doing this exercise, I tried to think about what students needed to learn first, next, and so on as I considered the learning they needed to obtain in order to demonstrate understanding and application of the full standard. This ended up being a brainstorming activity, as whenever I thought my list was complete, I would think of something else. The point is, the standard itself is deceptive—a lot of learning is embedded within the standard, as demonstrated. The process of thinking about what students really need to learn clarifies what stepping-stones will be required to get them to the destination.

The Formative Assessment Connection

The use of formative assessments in the classroom has received growing attention over the past 15 years, and rightfully so. This powerful classroom practice is best used in conjunction with learning progressions—the two go hand in hand. A learning progression is intended to provide the logical learning pathway(s) students will take in order to attain the larger curricular goal. In the example on time above, I have listed nine "subskills" and pieces of "enabling knowledge." This may result in one learning progression, or it may result in two or three. In your classroom, you may naturally decide at some point that you need to stop and check for understanding before continuing with instruction. You may be seeing some blank stares from students, or raised eyebrows, or students may be asking multiple questions. Whatever it is, you are triggered to stop, check for understanding, and adjust instruction instead of just plowing through. Such formative checks can reveal students' misconceptions early in the learning process, so they can be corrected before a gap becomes too great. When you have a learning progression, you purposefully plan where you will stop to formatively assess student understanding. Even when you take this deliberate action, of course, there will still be occasions when you get blank stares when you are not expecting them.

It should be noted that learning progressions have long been discussed in relation to formative assessment, going back to a 1998 study by Black and Wiliam. These researchers conclude that teachers need "more than good assessment instruments—they also need help to develop methods to interpret and respond to the results in a formative way" (p. 37). They go on to state: "One requirement for such an approach is a sound model of students' progression in the learning of the subject matter, so that the criteria that guide the formative strategy can be matched to students' trajectories in learning" (p. 37). It is only natural that learning progressions should be used in conjunction with formative assessments, which enable instructional adjustments based on the student feedback generated. The final destination remains the same, but the stepping-stones may need to be adjusted.

Heritage's (2010) formative assessment model commences with the development of the learning progression and ends with "closing the gap" (learning). Heritage notes that the formative assessment process "is intended to close the gap between where the learner currently is and where the learner and the teacher want to be at the end of the lesson. The idea of closing the 'gap' comes from D. Royce Sadler (1989), who stressed feedback as the centerpiece of formative assessment" (p. 10).

I am very fond of James Popham's work on assessment, in particular *Transformative Assessment* (2008). Popham defines formative assessment as "a planned process in which assessment-elicited evidence of students' status is used by teachers to adjust their ongoing instructional procedures or by students to adjust their current learning tactics" (p. 6). He stresses obtaining assessment-elicited evidence but also indicates that this does not always have to be pencil-and-paper evidence. The type of assessment selected is important, because it is necessary to gather valid evidence and enough evidence to make an accurate inference about a student's status. Learning progressions are an integral part of Popham's formative assessment process and an ongoing part of instruction. Accordingly, "to make formative assessment function most effectively, it is almost always necessary for teachers to employ learning progressions as the frameworks by which they can identify appropriate occasions for assessment-informed adjustment decisions. Learning progressions, in an almost literal sense, become the maps that provide guidance on how best to carry out formative assessment" (p. 29). Teachers may have a tendency to do this naturally, but the key is to make it more deliberate.

John Hattie's comprehensive and continually growing meta-analysis of influences on student learning and achievement place the effect size of feedback, which is at the center of the formative assessment process, at 0.73, which equates to almost two years of student achievement growth. All three of the education scholars cited above, some of the best known in the field, link learning progressions to the formative assessment process, both of which incorporate feedback.

You may be wondering what learning progressions have to do with developing performance tasks. Well, it all starts and ends with planning for instruction and assessment, because the process is the same. We are building the base, and learning progressions are a part of the base. They may drive the formative assessment process, but they also drive the development of the learning intentions and success criteria for the unit of instruction, which drive the performance task.

The Common Core State Standards and Learning Progressions

For each of the four strands of the ELA CCSS—Reading, Writing, Speaking and Listening, and Language—there are College and Career Readiness (CCR) anchor standards that represent the outcomes that will prepare students for either college or the workforce. The K–12 standards were purposefully developed to "define end-of-year expectations" and are "a cumulative progression designed to enable students to meet college and career readiness expectations no later than the end of high school" (Common Core State Standards Initiative, 2010a, p. 4). Each grade level has standards in the four strands that delineate the learning progress students should make. In essence, this is a learning progression over 13 years to attain the CCR anchor standards. Since the ELA CCSS standards are written as a K–12 learning progression, they do not delineate everything a student should know, understand, and be able to do each year.

Take a look at the first anchor standard in the Reading Standards for Literature in Table 3.1, in conjunction with the grade-level standards for grades 6, 7, and 8. The only difference between the sixth-grade standard and the seventh-grade standard is that in seventh grade students need to be able to cite "several pieces of textual evidence." As students move into eighth grade, they need to be able to make judgments as to what textual evidence best supports the analysis of the text.

The question comes down to this: What do students need to learn in each of these respective grades about analyzing a piece of literature and being able to cite evidence to support the analysis? It is understood that text complexity is increasing at each grade level, but beyond that, what do students need to know, understand, and do at each grade level? Since the nuances between the standards for the different grade levels are minuscule, it is necessary to dig deeper into what it is specifically students in each grade level should be responsible for learning and how they should demonstrate and apply their understanding when citing textual evidence, both explicit and inferential, in analyzing a piece of literature.

Table 3.1   CCSS Reading Standards for Literature Learning Progression, Grades 6–8

College and Career Readiness Anchor Standards for Reading			
Key Ideas and Details—Literature			
CCR Anchor Standard	*Grade 6*	*Grade 7*	*Grade 8*
1. Read closely to determine what the text says explicitly and to make logical inferences from it; cite specific textual evidence when writing or speaking to support conclusions drawn from the text.	1. Cite textual evidence to support analysis of what the text says explicitly as well as inferences drawn from the text.	1. Cite several pieces of textual evidence to support analysis of what the text says explicitly as well as inferences drawn from the text.	1. Cite the textual evidence that most strongly supports an analysis of what the text says explicitly as well as inferences drawn from the text.

The introduction to the Math CCSS document notes that "the development of these Standards began with research-based learning progressions detailing what is known today about how students' mathematical knowledge, skill, and understanding develop over time" (Common Core State Standards Initiative, 2010b, p. 4). There is a tiered organization to the Math CCSS, starting with common domains throughout grades K–8 and then course-specific standards as students move into high school. Under each domain at each grade level, the standard is delineated and then followed by a cluster, or grouping, of related standards that support attainment of the standard. As demonstrated by the example on time above, a lot of learning is embedded into each standard.

Know, Understand, Do

The acronym KUD—short for "know, understand, do"—has become commonplace in the planning of instruction and assessments. Thinking in terms of KUDs is helpful for educators in planning, instruction, and assessment because it delineates and clarifies what it is that students need to know, understand, and be able to do. Additionally, KUDs support the development of learning progressions. Kathy Tuchman Glass (2013) is a proponent of using KUDs in the development of CCSS curriculum maps, in particular for English language arts. KUDs can be developed for any subject area. The topic of KUDs is included in this chapter because KUDs can serve as a means to an end.

Know

The knowledge component of KUDs can be defined as "the factual information that students use as the foundation for gleaning overarching concepts; specifically, knowledge includes facts, dates, people, places, examples, and vocabulary/terms of a given unit" (Glass, 2013, p. 42). In the development of a learning progression, the knowledge tends to be the "enabling knowledge"—that is, the information, term, fact, or other knowledge that students need to know in order to attain the standard.

Every content area has knowledge that students need to master in order to attain different standards, and science and social studies are heavy in the knowledge department. The critical component to remember is the fact that knowledge builds from the lower to the upper grades. For instance, the topic of weather and climate is part of the Earth and Space Sciences section of the Next Generation Science Standards in the area of Earth's Systems. This topic is evident in elementary, middle, and high school, yet the knowledge students need to master varies greatly from lower to higher grades. In third grade, based on the ESS2-1 standard, weather knowledge might include knowledge of terms such as *precipitation, wind direction, pictograph,* and *bar graph.* Note that this standard could also be addressed within a math unit of instruction on measurement. Middle school weather and climate knowledge might include the terms *low pressure, high pressure, fronts, humidity,* and *barometric pressure.* Social studies would have similar variation, as typically the topics of study repeat themselves throughout the grade spans of elementary, middle, and high school, expanding upon the knowledge, understandings, and the skills students need to do. Knowledge in English language arts might entail story elements in the elementary grades, such as character, setting, and plot, and then as students progress to middle school, themes may be added, as well as the concepts of rising action and climax.

Next up in the discussion is the "do" of KUD. The *D* may be last in the acronym, but it goes hand in hand with the knowledge—students need both knowledge and skills. We will save the best for last: understand.

Do

When we discuss "doing" we are talking about skills and sub-skills. Just knowing something is not very useful; you have to be able to do something with that knowledge. However, if you are creating a KUD chart, you may list some skills that do not have accompanying knowledge (I will explain this shortly). What is nice is that both the ELA and the Math CCSS are written as performance standards, as you can see in Figure 3.1. The Next Generation Science Standards and the revised standards of the National Council for the Social Studies are also written as performance standards.

Let's take a deeper look at the sixth-grade ELA CCSS reading standard shown in Figure 3.1, which requires students to "cite textual evidence." A few subskills and skills come to mind that students will need to be able to have in order to cite textual evidence. First, a subskill would be to be able to identify textual evidence—students have to be able to identify it before they can actually cite it. There are different ways in which students might cite textual evidence. They could use direct quotes to do so, but that does not expand their learning beyond the fifth-grade outcome for this CCR anchor standard. Students at the sixth-grade level will need to cite evidence in either written or oral format. In either case, they could summarize or paraphrase in order to cite evidence. If you were completing a KUD chart to create a learning progression, you might include "summarize" as a skill.

Figure 3.1   Performance Standards From Four Core Subject Areas

Illinois Social Studies, Civic and Political Institutions, Moderately Complex (MdC), Grades 6–8

SS.CV.2.6-8.MdC Explain the origins, functions, and structure of government with reference to the U.S. Constitution, Illinois Constitution, and other systems of government.

Common Core State Standards, Mathematics, Measurement and Data, Grade 2

2.MD.7 Tell and write time from analog and digital clocks to the nearest five minutes, using a.m. and p.m.

Next Generation Science Standards, Earth and Space Sciences, Grade 3

3-ESS2-1 Represent data in tables and graphical displays to describe typical weather conditions expected during a particular season.

Common Core State Standards, English Language Arts, Reading/ Literature, Grade 6

RL.6.1 Cite textual evidence to support analysis of what the text says explicitly as well as inferences drawn from the text.

Understand

I have saved the "understand" component of KUD for last because students have to have knowledge and skills in order to arrive at understandings. Many phrases have been offered to help teachers get a better handle on the meaning of understandings. Understandings have been referenced as essential or enduring understandings, "Big Ideas," generalizations, and conceptual understandings. In *Understanding by Design,* Wiggins and McTighe (2005) devote an entire chapter to the comprehension of understanding; it is appropriately titled "Understanding Understanding." This chapter is very enlightening, and Wiggins and McTighe's clarification of an understanding is particularly useful:

> An *understanding* is the successful result of trying to understand—the resultant grasp of an *unobvious* idea, an inference that makes meaning of many discrete (and perhaps seemingly insignificant) elements of knowledge. (p. 43)

The most important aspect of understandings is that ideally you want students to discover them on their own, as a result of their learning of the knowledge and skills. Interestingly, understandings may change depending on the standards that are within a unit of study and how they interact. The understandings are the "aha moments" students have when they are learning and the lightbulb goes on. It's as if they are having an epiphany.

Let me share a story to help you better comprehend (I purposefully did not say understand) the concept of understanding. As a senior in college, back in the fall of 1985, I had the opportunity to participate in the Semester at Sea program, which was sponsored by the University of Pittsburgh. Students in the program took four courses over the semester, which met while we were on board a ship at sea between ports. Our trip left from Seattle, Washington, and in our travels we visited Japan, Korea, Hong Kong, mainland China, Sri Lanka, India, Egypt, Israel, Turkey, Greece, and Spain. After visiting the four Asian countries, I had an "aha moment." In Japan the main mode of transportation was the bullet train. In Korea, the moped and a small car, like a Kia, were the main transportation choices. I remember being amazed that a family of four with two small children could ride on a moped. In Hong Kong, we walked everywhere we went. Finally, in China (and please remember this was more than 30 years ago), the roads that were wide, like three-lane highways in the United States, were filled with bicyclists. On either side of these bicycle roads were smaller access roads used by only handfuls of cars. My "aha" was that the geography and economic status of the country determined the mode of transportation. I was observing factual information and arrived at an understanding that I discovered because of my own learning and experiences. My economics professor on the ship never mentioned anything about transportation. One of the characteristics of understanding that Wiggins and McTighe (2005) discuss is that understanding is all about transfer—that is, taking the knowledge, concepts, and/or skills you have learned and applying them to new situations. Transfer can be challenging for maturing learners.

John Hattie (2009, 2012) discusses surface, deep, and conceptual levels of understanding. Surface learning equates to basic knowledge, such as facts and information. The shift from surface to deep learning takes place when the learner makes connections and extensions among the facts and information. As Hattie (2012) notes, "surface and deep understanding lead to the student developing conceptual understanding" (p. 54), which involves transfer. In her book *Concept-Based Curriculum and Instruction for the Thinking Classroom*, H. Lynn Erickson (2007) emphasizes conceptual thinking as the vehicle for deeper levels of understanding as a result of transfer:

> Conceptual thinking requires the ability to critically examine factual information; relate to prior knowledge; see patterns and connections; draw out significant understandings at the conceptual level; evaluate the truth of the understandings based on the supporting evidence; transfer the understanding across time or situation; and, often, use the conceptual understanding to creatively solve a problem or create a new product, process, or idea. (p. 19)

You may be thinking, "Why do teachers have to come up with what students need to understand (KUD), when students need to arrive at their own understandings?" Students may arrive at their own understandings based on their prior knowledge and how they see the knowledge, but teachers need to be cognizant of the deeper (conceptual) understandings, so that their instruction can target those understandings. Students then will have the ability to transfer their deeper understandings to new situations. As Wiggins and McTighe (2005) note:

> With deliberate and explicit instruction in how to transfer (and assessments that constantly demand such transfer), the learner must take what were initially bits of knowledge with no clear structure or power and come to see them as part of a larger, more meaningful, and more useful system. Without lessons designed to bring ideas to life, concepts such as honor, manifest destiny, or the water cycle remain empty phrases to be memorized, depriving learners of the realization that ideas have power. (p. 43)

Understandings are a critical component, not only for KUDs but also for learning progressions.

KUDs can be useful tools in the development of learning progressions. A KUD chart may have all the pertinent components, but it does *not* delineate a learning pathway that students might take to progress their learning to attain the standard. Earlier in this chapter, to make the point that a learning progression further clarifies and targets what needs to be learned, I used the CCSS mathematics standard 2.MD.7. Figures 3.2 and 3.3 show the transition from KUD chart to learning progression.

Figure 3.2   KUD Chart for Grade 2 on Time

KNOW	UNDERSTAND	DO
• ¾ hour	Time dictates our lives.	• Tell time (to the ¼ hour, ¾ hour, nearest 5 minutes on both styles of clocks)
• ¼ hour	Time never stops.	
• noon		• State (number of hours in a day)
• midnight	*The knowledge includes "enabling knowledge." It goes beyond the language in the standard.*	
• a.m.		• Write time (¼ hour, ¾ hour, 5 minutes)
• p.m.		• Identify (hours of a.m., p.m.)
• along	*Note that each verb indicates the knowledge allowing for easy transfer to a learning progression.*	• Explain (the relationships between a.m., p.m., noon, and midnight)
• digital		
• intervals of 5		
• hours in a day	*The "subskill" of count needs to be in place before telling time.*	• Round (to the nearest 5 minutes)
• rounding up		
• rounding down		• Count (intervals of 5 to 60)

Figure 3.3   Learning Progression for Grade 2 on Time

2.MD.7 Tell and write time from analog and digital clocks to the nearest five minutes, using a.m. and p.m.

Learning Progressions	Subskills and Skills	Enabling Knowledge (information, facts) and Concepts
	State	Number of hours in a day
	Identify	Hours of a.m. and p.m.
	Explain	The relationships between noon, midnight, a.m., and p.m.
	Formative Checkpoint—Checking for Understanding	
	Count	By 5s to 60
	Write	Time to ¼ hour, ¾ hour, using a.m./p.m., on analog and digital clocks
	Tell	Time to ¼ hour, ¾ hour, using a.m./p.m., on analog and digital clocks
	Formative Checkpoint—Checking for Understanding	
	Round	Up and down between 5 and 60
	Round	To the nearest five minutes
	Tell	Time to the nearest five minutes on analog and digital clocks
	Write	Time to the nearest five minutes on analog and digital clocks
	Formative Checkpoint—Checking for Understanding	
Conceptual understandings	Time dictates our lives.	
	Time never stops.	

> There are actually three learning progressions present. I grouped subskills and enabling knowledge together and determined where I would formatively check for student understanding.

> Note that the conceptual understandings have been placed at the ends of the learning progressions.

Honoring Other Educational Processes

By including a KUD chart as a means to create a learning progression, I do not mean to diminish the importance of other well-known processes that schools and districts might utilize that can serve the same purpose as KUDs. There are several processes of planning instruction in which the standards are dissected, deconstructed, or whatever term you would like to use, with the aim of determining the knowledge, understandings, and skills that students need for particular units of instruction. Let's take a look at a few of these, as there is no sense in reinventing the wheel if you already have curricular documents that get at the essence of what students need to know, understand, and do.

"Unwrapping" the Standards

One approach is the process of "unwrapping" the standards in conjunction with determining Big Ideas and essential questions. Larry Ainsworth has written extensively on the unwrapping process, including Big Ideas and essential questions, dating back to his first book on the topic, *"Unwrapping" the Standards: A Simple Process to Make Standards Manageable* (2003). The Big Ideas equate to the "understandings" of KUDs. This process continues to be a major component in Ainsworth's latest book, *Common Formative Assessments 2.0* (2015), and developing learning progressions is now a part of the process as well. The unwrapping process involves identifying the concepts and skills within the actual standards. The concepts represent what students need to know, and the skills represent what students need to be able to do with the knowledge, but the concepts and skills are drawn *solely* from what is written in the standard. The Big Ideas are the conceptual understandings that are generated from the "unwrapped" concepts and skills and are accompanied by essential questions, which are intended to guide or lead students to discover the Big Ideas on their own. If you are familiar with this process, you might be able to use it as a starting point for developing learning progressions.

Understanding by Design

Grant Wiggins and Jay McTighe (2005) became very well known for their Understanding by Design (UbD) model of developing units of instruction and curriculum design. There are three stages to their backward design model. The first stage, identifying desired results, is the starting point in the UbD process; the desired results, or established goals, could be standards, course objectives, or outcomes. The next stage involves identifying what students need to understand about the established goals. Understandings occur when students grapple with the knowledge, which basically consists of facts and concepts, through reflection, application, and inquiry. What can students discover about the knowledge that makes it important? The UbD process also has essential questions, which Wiggins and McTighe state should be "provocative questions" that "foster inquiry, understanding, and transfer of learning" (p. 22). The final stage of this process involves identifying what students will know and what they will be able to do. The goal is to bring clarity to what students are learning. Once again, this process is a version of identifying KUDs.

Concept-Based Curriculum

Concept-based curriculum design is based on the extensive work of H. Lynn Erickson (2007). According to Erickson, curriculum models have typically been two-dimensional, focusing on what students need to know and what they can do. A concept-based curriculum model is three-dimensional, with the third dimension consisting of what students need to understand. In this model the factual level of thinking works in conjunction with the conceptual level of thinking to promote "intellectual development." Erickson's approach and her research match those of John Hattie, who encourages educators to move beyond surface learning to deep learning and conceptual learning. When curriculum and instruction require students to process factual information through the conceptual level of thinking, the students demonstrate greater retention of factual information, deeper levels of understanding, and increased motivation for learning.

In developing a unit of instruction using the concept-based model, you start with your topic and, of course, your academic standards and then determine a "lens" through which to study the topic, such as change, revolution, or patterns. According to Erickson, this lens enables the learner to make the connections between the factual and conceptual understandings. Next, you need to identify the critical content, which is what students need to know about the topic, as well as the skills they need to be able to do. You must then determine the concepts for the unit, which are derived from the critical content. Erickson (2007) defines concepts as "mental constructs that 'umbrella' different topical examples and meet these criteria: timeless, universal, abstract (to different degrees), different examples that share common attributes" (p. 31). From this point, generalizations are determined based on the relationships of two or more of the concepts. These are the enduring understandings, or the big takeaways, about the content. To take a two-dimensional learning outcome that has content and a verb, such as "Compare the attributes of a fable to those of myth," and make it into a three-dimensional format, Erickson suggests extending the statement, using the phrase "in order to understand that" (p. 7). An example would be "Compare the attributes of a fable to those of a myth *in order to understand that* there are different types of writing and each has its own attributes or characteristics in order to convey its message." The second part of the sentence is the enduring understanding, what you want students to take away from comparing the attributes of a fable from those of a myth. If you have followed Erickson's work in your classroom, school, or district, you already have a good starting place for developing learning progressions.

Building the Base Step 2: Determine Learning Progressions

Taking ideas from both James Popham's (2008) and Margaret Heritage's (2010) work on learning progressions, here is my spin on how to go about developing a learning progression, broken down into four steps. This needs to be a process that is user-friendly for teachers and instructional coaches, so my intent is to avoid making it too complex. You will have to use your judgment, based on the curricular documents you currently have in your school, district, or state, in determining what parts of the process you can and cannot complete.

1. Begin with a thorough understanding of each of the primary standards in the unit of study and what it is students in your grade level specifically need to know, understand, and be able to do. Creating a KUD will be helpful if you are not familiar with another process for this purpose, such as unwrapping the standards or Understanding by Design.

2. Identify the enabling knowledge and subskills that students need to learn in order to progress toward or attain the learning outcomes, depending on the time of the school year. For example, what students need to know, understand, and be able to do in respect to writing an argument changes from September to March. What do students need to learn first, second, third, and so on? I recommend that you address each standard individually as you determine the enabling knowledge and subskills, and then, as the learning progressions are established, they may be intertwined or remain separate. Each piece of enabling knowledge will be associated with a subskill, because you have to be able to do something with each piece of enabling knowledge. Heritage (2010) suggests writing the skills and the kinds of knowledge on sticky notes, so as you discuss and collaborate with other teachers in developing the learning progression, based on your experiences with students and knowledge of learning, you can manipulate the notes into the most likely instructional sequence.

3. Ensure that each learning progression segment can be measured. This is where formative assessment comes into play. You should be monitoring student progress on the learning progressions, so students can adjust their learning tactics and you can adjust instruction. It is not necessary to formatively

assess each and every segment of a learning progression; segments could be grouped together, as shown in Figure 3.3.

4. Place the enabling knowledge and subskills in the order you and your colleagues deem best for students' learning, based on research and your experience as teachers and learners. Make a note in each place in the order where you want to check for understanding. The concepts and skills that fall above such a checkpoint are considered a learning progression.

These four steps will start your journey toward developing learning progressions to enhance your classroom instructional practices. Popham (2008) does not mince words in his writing; thus, it seems apt here to share his reminder about learning progressions:

Be sure to remember that any learning progression you develop, however well thought out and carefully constructed, is incapable of being anything but your best-guess hypothesis of the sequenced precursors that lead, step by step, to students' mastery of an important curricular aim. First-version learning progressions frequently need some serious reworking, and you will need to keep a close watch on any learning progression you develop to see, over time, whether it seems to be appropriate. (p. 41)

At this point, the base has been strengthened and what students need to learn in order to attain the year-end outcomes is gaining clarity. The learning progressions that are developed in this phase of building the base take on a new level of meaning in Chapter 4, which concludes the building of the base and brings us closer to the development of a performance task.

Follow Along: Creating a Performance Task

We continue to build the base by clarifying the standards (destinations) in the unit through developing a learning progression for each primary standard in the unit. Essentially it comes down to figuring out what students need to know (bodies of enabling knowledge), understand, and be able to do (subskills) in order to attain the standard and then creating the most reasonable sequence through which students can learn the knowledge, understandings, and skills.

The performance task template in Appendix 1 includes a learning progression chart in Step 2; if you need to utilize a KUD chart first, create a template similar to the one in Figure 3.2. You can complete the process without doing a KUD chart, but if you are more comfortable creating one first, by all means do so. You may want to try doing it both ways to determine which works best for you. Figure 3.4 presents a social studies example for one particular standard that you can reference as you are completing your own learning progression.

1. Either create a KUD chart and write down what students need to know, understand, and be able to do for each standard or ask yourself the question, "For this particular standard, what is everything I need to teach students?" Write each skill and piece of knowledge or concept on a sticky note, one skill or concept per note. For example, "List the three branches of government" and "Explain the function of each branch of government." This will allow you to manipulate the skills and concepts as you work to place them in the most logical order for instruction.

Figure 3.4   Virginia and U.S. History Learning Progression, CE.2.a

CE.2 The student will apply social science skills to understand the foundations of American constitutional government by
   a.   explaining the fundamental principles of consent of the governed, limited government, rule of law, democracy, and representative government.

Learning Progression	*Subskills and Skills*	*Enabling Knowledge (information, facts) and Concepts*
	Define/describe	Consent of the governed
	Define/describe	Limited government
	Define/describe	Rule of law
	Formatively Checking for Understanding	
	Define/describe	Representative government
	Define/describe	Democracy
	Formatively Checking for Understanding	
Understandings: "This is important to learn because . . ."	American constitutional government is based on fundamental political principles that go back over two centuries.	
	These fundamental principles are present in our daily lives as U.S. citizens.	

Figure 3.5 Skill/Concept for Learning Progression

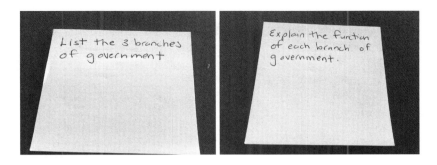

2. Once you have all your sticky notes written out, begin the process of placing them in the instructional sequence you think is the most logical for students. The number of notes you have will determine whether you will have more than one learning progression. The ending point for a learning progression is the point at which you purposefully check for understanding before continuing with instruction. Discuss with your colleagues and study the research to create what your team deems to be the best instructional sequence. There is no right or wrong order, because not all students will follow the same learning path. The learning progression is your collective best hypothesis.

3. Once you have finalized the order of your sticky notes, transfer the skills and concepts to the learning progression chart, Step 2 on the performance task template. If you have more than one learning progression for the standard, place a shaded area between them that indicates this is a "formative checkpoint," where you will be checking for understanding (see examples in Figures 3.3 and 3.4). In the social studies example in Figure 3.4, the teacher will formatively check for understanding after teaching three skills and concepts, before progressing to the final two.

Key Takeaways

- Learning progressions have been defined in many ways. James Popham's (2008) definition and work are emphasized throughout this chapter. His definition of a learning progression is "a sequenced set of subskills and bodies of enabling knowledge that, it is believed, students must master en route to mastering a more remote curricular aim" (p. 24).

- There are three common agreements on learning progressions:
  1. They describe key junctions in student learning that are intended to close the gap between present and intended learning.
  2. They should be based on evidence from research and practitioner observation.
  3. They are never perfectly constructed, as there are too many variables across learners.
- Learning progressions serve to focus the lens to target student learning more precisely.
- Learning progressions allow you to purposefully plan for formative assessment through checking for understanding by some means.
- The ELA CCSS are written as a learning progression, but individual teachers need to further define the standards, as the differences between grade levels are minuscule in many instances.
- The KUD (know, understand, do) chart is one means of breaking down the standards, but it is not the only process available.

Reflection Questions

1. Which definition of learning progression works best with your understanding? What draws you to this definition?

2. What in this chapter captured your interest the most? Why do you think that was the case?

3. Besides enabling teachers to target student learning more precisely and to purposefully decide on formative assessment checkpoints, do learning progressions offer other benefits that you can see? If so, what are those benefits?

4. Which process for digging deeper into the primary standards do you prefer and why?

5. Do you recognize the benefits of using learning progressions? Why or why not?

6. What resonated with you the most in this chapter and why?

4

Building the Base

Going SOLO!

W̲e started our process with the identification of standards within a unit of study, and then we dug deeper into each of the standards to discover exactly what it is that students need to learn in order to successfully demonstrate understanding and application of the respective standards. We then placed the things that students need to know and be able to do in a learning progression, the sequence deemed to be the most reasonable learning pathway for the students. Now it is time to determine the learning intentions and accompanying success criteria for the unit, and in doing so, we will utilize the SOLO (structure of the observed learning outcome) model. We are "going SOLO" to create the strongest base possible as we plan instructional learning experiences and formative and summative assessments.

Targeted Learning: One Step Closer to Clarity

The learning progressions that we have created are the building blocks for learning intentions and success criteria, which take clarity of learning to the next level. Think of learning intentions and success criteria as a happily married couple who have been together for 50-plus years. We often hear that when one partner in such a marriage passes away, the other is likely to pass shortly thereafter, as was the case with my aunt Pat, who died about two weeks after my uncle Frank in 2005. They were married for 57 years. The point is that learning intentions can't survive without their success criteria. These two components, which help to focus learning in the classroom (Hattie, 2012), have to be together to be vital and alive. In *The Focus Model*, B. R. Jones (2014) addresses how learning intentions and success criteria work together to provide clarity for both teachers and students. They bring clarity to "three things: what needs to be learned, how the learning is progressing, and once learning is measured, what are the next steps for both teachers and students in the learning process" (p. 42). Hattie speaks to teacher clarity in *Visible Learning* (2009), noting that it has an effect size of 0.75. Teachers should communicate the learning intentions and success criteria for lessons and units to the students, essentially making them visible. As part of the planning process, teachers should determine the learning intentions of units and lessons as well as the accompanying success criteria. Then, by simply communicating these intentions and success criteria to the students, so they are aware of what they are learning and know when they have successfully met the learning intentions, teachers are on their way to developing assessment-capable learners and positively influencing student achievement by almost two years. It is amazing how such a commonsense action can have such a dramatic impact on student progress and achievement.

Learning Intentions and Success Criteria Defined and Explained

In basic terms, learning intentions describe what it is you intend students to learn in a unit or lesson; success criteria describe how students will know they have achieved the intended learning intention (Hattie, 2012). As Hattie (2009) explains:

> Learning intentions describe what it is we want students to learn in terms of the skills, knowledge, attitudes, and values within any particular unit or lesson. Learning intentions should be clear, and provide guidance to the teacher about what to teach, help learners be aware of what they should learn from the lesson, and form the basis for assessing what the students have learnt and for assessing what the teachers have taught well to each student. (pp. 162–163)

Learning intentions are derived from the standards, but remember, a standard by itself does not include everything students need to know, understand, and be able to do, as pointed out in Chapter 3. Thus, in building the final phase of the base for your performance task, you will be utilizing learning progressions in conjunction with the standards to determine learning intentions. The terms *learning objectives, learning outcomes,* or *learning goals* might be more common vernacular in your district. However, my preference is *learning intentions,* because it emphasizes what is intended for the student to learn—it does not mean the student has learned it. Think of the learning intentions as the checkpoints on the way to the final destination (the standard). The success criteria tell you when you have arrived at the destination.

As mentioned earlier, success criteria and learning intentions are basically joined at the hip, like an old married couple. It is when they are together, as one, that they have the most influence on student achievement. Simply stated, success criteria define what it takes to attain the learning intentions, and students need to know up front what it takes to be successful in order to be engaged in the learning. What is it that defines success for a student whose learning intention is to tell and write time from analog and digital clocks to the nearest five-minute mark?

The success criteria serve as guideposts for student learning. In the words of John Hattie (2012), supporting Shirley Clarke's position:

> We must not make the mistake of making success criteria relate merely to completing the activity or a lesson having been engaging and enjoyable; instead the major role is to get the students engaged in and enjoying the challenge of learning. It is challenge that keeps us invested in pursuing goals and committed to achieving goals. (p. 51)

Clarke (2001, 2008) and Hattie (2012) are both proponents of student-created success criteria, as helping to develop their own criteria gets students more actively involved in their learning as well as increases commitment to the learning. Students can easily respond to the question "How will we know that you have attained (learned) the learning intention?" or "What does it take to be successful in meeting the learning intention?" Through her extensive work in schools on formative assessment and the use of learning intentions and success criteria, Clarke has discovered that for optimal impact, success criteria should be generated by the students. A practice that is common with written products is to show an example of a finished product from the previous year (or one the teacher created if a student-created one is not available) and guide a discussion of why the product meets the learning intentions. Another version of this is to show two examples of the same product, one of which meets the success criteria and one of which does not (Clarke, 2008). Recorded oral presentations from previous years could also be used, or you could be creative and have a student model and record an oral presentation for the purpose of creating the success criteria. Prior to engaging students in generating the success criteria for a learning intention, the teacher should determine the success criteria, so that he or she can guide the classroom discussion in case students overlook something important. Success criteria are related to scoring guides, but success criteria are set up basically as a checklist, whereas scoring guides include levels of quality.

Important Aspects of Learning Intentions and Success Criteria

Several key aspects of learning intentions can help make them powerful contributors to student learning. When you are planning and implementing learning intentions and success criteria, you should target learning, communicate the learning intentions and success criteria to students, and avoid including the learning context.

Target Learning

Learning intentions, in conjunction with success criteria, are the catalyst behind instruction and assessment and thus behind performance tasks. They target the learning. Remember, learning intentions and success criteria are like a happily married couple, and between their wedding day and death, life occurs—with a family, jobs, happiness, and sadness—just as instruction and assessment occur between the learning intentions and the success criteria. The success criteria can be met either through learning experiences or through formative or summative assessments—and in all cases these could be performance tasks.

Communicate Learning Intentions and Success Criteria

Communicating learning intentions and success criteria to students does not just mean posting them on the whiteboard. They should be discussed so students understand what they are learning and why, as well as when they are successful in meeting the success criteria. It has become common practice across the country, ever since standards became mandatory in every state, for teachers to post learning intentions or outcomes for lessons, or series of lessons, on bulletin boards, whiteboards, sentence strips, or chalkboards. Elementary classrooms throughout the United States have one or two learning intentions (objectives, outcomes) posted for each subject area. Secondary school classrooms display learning intentions as well, but focused typically on their respective subject areas. Yet success criteria for the learning intentions are not evident in the majority of elementary, middle, or high schools. So, when students see on the board "Today we are learning to tell time to the nearest five minutes," they know what they are learning, but they don't know what it will take for them to be successful. In this case, students are aiming at a moving target, guessing what success would look like. The learning intention and the success criteria have gotten a divorce.

However, to be fair, *success criteria* has not been a familiar term in U.S. education. Teachers are more familiar with rubrics and scoring guides, and it took time for that familiarity to grow. As noted above, scoring guides are not the same as success criteria. Success criteria play an integral role in the development of scoring guides, however, which are discussed in depth in Chapter 6.

How can students be successful if they don't know what success looks like? Teacher clarity, with an effect size of 0.75, is about communicating learning intentions (what students need to learn) and success criteria (what students need to do to demonstrate that they have learned what was intended). As part of this communication it is also important to revisit the learning intentions during and at the end of the unit or lesson to reinforce the learning (Clarke, 2001; Hattie, 2012). Informing students of the learning intentions should not be a one-shot deal at the beginning of a unit or lesson. Open communication in the classroom brings students into the learning process and improves student achievement and engagement in what they are learning and their progress in meeting the success criteria.

Avoid Including the Learning Context

Another critical element that Clarke (2001, 2008) stresses in regard to the writing of learning intentions is the need to avoid including the context, as the focus ends up being on the activity versus the learning.

The learning context can best be described as the activity students are doing as part of the learning. Compare these two types of learning intentions:

- Learning intention with context:
  - o Today we are learning to identify types of basketball passes by watching NCAA game clips.
  - o Today we are learning to pass the basketball to team members.
- Learning intention without context:
  - o Today we are learning to identify types of basketball passes.
  - o Today we are learning to pass the basketball.

In addition, the success criteria should be applicable to different contexts, not just the context of the present learning experience, and such limitations often occur when learning intentions and context mix company. The focus on learning becomes cloudy. For example:

- Success criteria with context:
  - o We are successful when we are able to identify three types of passes from NCAA clips.
  - o We are successful when we are able to pass the basketball, on at least three occasions, to a player on our team while being guarded.
- Success criteria without context:
  - o We are successful when we are able to identify three types of passes.
  - o We are successful when we are able to pass the basketball using one of the three types of passes.

For further clarification, consider the following scenario. Mrs. Murdoch, a high school English teacher, has been working with the local Veterans of Foreign Wars (VFW) post to arrange for students in her senior honors English class to interview 18 veterans who served overseas for the United States during wars or other conflicts. The students will interview the veterans, conduct some additional research on the conflicts the veterans served in, and then write historical short stories that incorporate information from the interviews and their research. The class has just finished reading Michael Chabon's novel *The Amazing Adventures of Kavalier & Clay*, which is set in New York City in the late 1930s, at a time when comic books were becoming the latest rage in America. The primary standards for the unit of study are shown below, and the focus during the reading of the book has been on the first two CCSS Reading Standards for Literature listed. The remaining three standards listed are incorporated into the performance task of writing a historical fiction short story.

Unit of Study: Historical Fiction

RL.11.12.2 Determine two or more themes or central ideas of a text and analyze their development over the course of the text, including how they interact and build on one another to produce a complex account; provide an objective summary of the text.

RL.11.12.3 Analyze the impact of the author's choices regarding how to develop and relate elements of a story or drama (e.g., where a story is set, how the action is ordered, how the characters are introduced and developed).

SL.11.12.5 Evaluate a speaker's point of view, reasoning, and use of evidence and rhetoric, assessing the stance, premises, links among ideas, word choice, points of emphasis, and tone used.

RI.11.12.7 Integrate and evaluate multiple sources of information presented in different media or formats (e.g., visually, quantitatively) as well as in words in order to address a question or solve a problem.

W.11.12.3 Write narratives to develop real or imagined experiences or events using effective technique, relevant descriptive details, and well-structured event sequences.

This is how Mrs. Murdoch started the class the day after the students finished reading the novel, with excitement in her voice and a smile on her face:

> We have finished reading *The Amazing Adventures of Kavalier & Clay*, and today we are going to transition to writing our own historically based short story. You will not just be conducting research for your historical fiction text, you will be interviewing a veteran from the local VFW who has served overseas and was involved in war or conflict. I have arranged for the interviews to take place in two days, and that doesn't leave us much time to prepare. Today we will learn how to evaluate a speaker's point of view, along with how the person expresses

his or her view and supports it with evidence, so you can make the most of your interviews with your veterans. You need to be well prepared to ask interview questions, including follow-up questions, as well as to listen attentively to your veterans and evaluate what they are saying and how they say it. Preparing our interview questions will be the focus of our learning tomorrow.

Where do you think the students' focus is at this point? I can visualize the buzz going on among students as they think about what conflicts the veterans served in and wonder if they were injured. The students will be learning how to evaluate any speaker's point of view and reasoning, not just a veteran's. As Clarke (2008) notes: "If you make clear which is the learning objective and which is the context, pupils are able to transfer skills within and across subjects. Instead of having to start again just because you've changed the context, pupils remember the last time the skill was used and can transfer it to a new and different context" (p. 87). These are seniors, and they should have been introduced to these standards in 11th grade, as the 9–12 CCSS in ELA are in two-year grade spans. If learning intentions are void of a context, students should be able to transfer their learning to a new context. How do you think Mrs. Murdoch could have presented both the learning intention for the lesson and the fact the students will be interviewing veterans separately so the activity of doing the interviews would not take center stage, taking emphasis away from learning to evaluate a speaker's point of view and reasoning?

Here is a little experiment you can try, either in your own classroom or in cooperation with another teacher. If you are an administrator or instructional coach, you could visit several classrooms. Ask several students in the classroom(s) these two questions: "What are you learning?" and "How will you know when you have learned it?" The students should not just be reading something from the board; rather, they should be talking to you, demonstrating that they completely understand what they are learning and that they are clear on the expectations for how they will show when they have learned it. What do the data collected in this experiment reveal about your communication of learning intentions and success criteria? Are students telling you what they are doing versus what they are learning? Are you being clear about the learning, or are students focusing on the activity (context)? You need to start by communicating the learning intentions and success criteria if you want your students to become assessment-capable learners who are actively engaged in their learning and can answer the three big questions: "Where am I going?"; "How am I going?"; and "Where to next?"

Teaching and learning should be a collaborative effort between students and teacher. Teachers should teach and learn with students, and sharing the learning intentions and success criteria is the first step in making the shift from students who are passive receptacles to students who are engaged and excited learners, involved and active in their learning.

The bottom line is that when you are writing your learning intentions and success criteria, you should be careful not to include the context within the wording of either. The context will come into play a little later in the process, as context is of critical importance when it comes to performance tasks.

Elements of Learning Intentions and Success Criteria

When it comes to writing learning intentions and accompanying success criteria, five major elements need to be taken into consideration: challenge, commitment, confidence, student expectations, and conceptual understanding (Hattie, 2012). Obviously, some of these have connections to the important aspects of learning intentions previously discussed. Additionally, when the SOLO taxonomy is used in the writing of learning intentions and success criteria, these elements should be included as best they can.

To begin with the first of these five elements, learning intentions and success criteria need to have an appropriate amount of *challenge* in relation to the task. As an example, consider the CCSS grade 8 geometry strands "Understand and apply the Pythagorean Theorem" (8.G.6.8). This is a new concept being introduced to eighth-grade students, so for most students there will be new learning, although a few might have some prior knowledge of the theorem. The challenge can't be too difficult, or students will become disengaged and want to give up or not even try. The challenge can't be too easy, either, because students will become bored and thus disengaged. It is like the Goldilocks effect—the challenge has to be just right. The 2009 High School Survey of Student Engagement found that only 48% of respondents were academically challenged in "most" or "all" of their classes, and 63% indicated that they did not have to work hard in any or up to two of their classes (Yazzie-Mintz, 2010). These are disappointing findings, indicating that we are doing a disservice to students, failing to prepare them to be college and career ready. In light of these data, ensuring that our learning intentions and success criteria have an appropriate amount of challenge, taking into consideration the students' prior knowledge and achievement and their belief in their ability to meet the challenge (self-efficacy), is an important part of the planning process. Another interesting aspect of challenge is that teachers view the task itself as challenging, whereas students see the challenge as how difficult it is to complete the task (Hattie, 2012). Students tend to think about the depth of their understanding that they need to apply to the task, while teachers try to make the task itself challenging for each student.

A second element that should be taken into consideration in respect to learning intentions and success criteria is that of *commitment*. Commitment is associated with the learning experiences that are planned as a result of the learning intentions and success criteria. These learning experiences need to be relevant and engaging yet remain challenging. It is the challenge that drives a student to be committed to the learning (Hattie, 2012), but relevance of learning also drives commitment. When students see the relevance in learning to write an argument, they will have more commitment to the learning. So, when you are communicating your learning intentions and success criteria, make sure that you speak to the relevance of the learning. Do not include the relevance in the written learning intentions or success criteria, but verbally share with students at some point why the learning is important. What is the benefit to students in learning "X" as part of their preparation for college, career, or life?

A third element to consider when you are writing learning intentions and success criteria is that of student *confidence*. The learning intentions and success criteria should build on students' confidence. When students have confidence that they can be successful in attaining the learning intentions, they are strengthening their resilience (Hattie, 2012). When students are faced with difficult situations, whether learning or personal, they recognize how to handle such situations as a result of their increased confidence.

A fourth element that should be taken into account in the writing of learning intentions and success criteria is *student expectations*, meaning the ability of students to predict their achievement accurately. Most students are very adept at predicting how well they will do. The one caution regarding this element is that some students may set their expectations lower than what they are really capable of doing (Hattie, 2012). These students may not have confidence in their learning ability or may be shying away from the challenge. From a teaching perspective, providing "opportunities for students to be involved in predicting their performance; clearly, making the learning intentions and success criteria transparent, having high, but appropriate, expectations, and providing feedback at the appropriate levels is critical to building confidence in successfully taking on challenging tasks" (Hattie, 2012, pp. 53–54). It is a tall order to fill, but a necessary one to enhance student learning.

The final element that should be considered in the writing of learning intentions and success criteria is *conceptual understanding*. Understanding can be divided into three levels: surface, deep, and conceptual. To get to the conceptual level of understanding, a student needs to have a combination of surface-level and deep understanding. When it comes to writing learning intentions and success criteria, you can target all three levels of understanding by utilizing the SOLO taxonomy (Hattie, 2012; Martin, 2011), which is why I have selected this taxonomy for discussion over Bloom's taxonomy or Webb's Depth of Knowledge scale.

At this point, you should have an understanding of learning intentions and success criteria, some of the important aspects of learning intentions, and the five elements to consider when writing learning intentions and success criteria. Now it is time to write some learning intentions and success criteria, and to do this we will be using the SOLO taxonomy.

The SOLO Taxonomy: Surface, Deep, and Conceptual Understanding

Well-written learning intentions include a balance of surface learning intentions and deep learning intentions, so students can be stretched to construct their own understandings by melding their surface and deep learning to reach the level of conceptual understanding (Hattie, 2009). Typically, most assessment questions, as well as questions in the classroom on a daily basis, tend to be surface-level questions, with occasional relational-level questions added to the mix. The goal should be to have a balance between the surface and the deep. It is recommended to start with a minimum of 30% surface and 30% deep, with the remaining 40% a combination of surface and deep. How do your classroom and assessment questions compare to these percentages? Students need to have a solid understanding of the surface learning in order to move into the deeper levels of understanding

(Hattie, 2012). Only when they can draw upon both surface and deep understanding are they able to grapple with conceptual understanding. The SOLO taxonomy is a planning tool for learning intentions and success criteria that helps to provide the needed balance of surface and deep understanding.

The Presence of SOLO

It is time for the United States to embrace the SOLO taxonomy as New Zealand, Australia, England, Denmark, and a number of other countries have over the past two decades. Bloom's taxonomy and its revised version, Webb's Depth of Knowledge (DOK) taxonomy, and the SOLO taxonomy are the most commonly used taxonomies in the United States. Bloom's was the predominant taxonomy in the United States for a number of decades, but Webb's DOK now seems to have surpassed it in popularity. If a resource uses Bloom's taxonomy, typically it also includes Webb's DOK as an option. The SOLO taxonomy is becoming more and more prevalent in the United States as schools, districts, and states are recognizing how valuable Hattie's visible learning program is to improving student learning and achievement.

I have chosen the SOLO taxonomy here over Bloom's taxonomy and Webb's DOK because both Bloom's and Webb's taxonomies are typically used for instructional planning and assessment questions. They assume that the level of rigor of the verb associated with the learning outcome is the same as the level of response produced by the student (Jones, 2014). However, that is not always the case. The student response could demonstrate understanding at the unistructural, multistructural, relational, or extended abstract levels, or even at the prestructural level, indicating no understanding, even if the question was at a relational level. For instance, consider the following student response to the assessment prompt "Justify [relational level] the need for the separation of powers in the United States government": "The United States government consists of the executive branch, legislative branch and judicial branch. Each branch of government has its own set of responsibilities. The executive branch includes the president and his/her role is to carry out the roles. The legislative role consists of the Senate and House of Representatives. They make the laws. The judicial branch evaluates the laws. There are nine Supreme Court judges." If this is the complete response, it is at the multistructural level, as it is primarily a description of each of the branches, with no connections made between the branches and no explanation given as to why the different roles are needed.

The Development of SOLO

John Biggs and Kevin Collis developed the SOLO (structure of the observed learning outcome) taxonomy in the 1970s and 1980s to observe and measure the quality of students' thinking along a continuum that starts at a concrete level and moves to an abstract level. They created the taxonomy to provide teachers (as well as students) with a means for evaluating *"how much* has been learned and *how well* it has been learned" as the result of learning and applying the "facts, skills, concepts, or problem-solving strategies" that were taught (Biggs & Collis, 1982, p. 3). The taxonomy is used to evaluate student responses at a given point of time; responses can be at one of five levels: prestructural, unistructural, multistructural, relational, and extended abstract.

It is important to understand that each level is based on four characteristics, which become progressively more complex as the levels increase: capacity, relating operation, consistency and closure, and structure. *Capacity* refers to the amount of working memory that is needed for each of the SOLO levels, whereas *relating operation* concerns how the prompt and the response "interrelate." *Consistency and closure* refers to two conflicting needs of the learner: The learner needs to respond to the prompt and come to closure, and at the same time needs to have consistency between the prompt and the response. The final characteristic is *structure,* which involves the visual representation of the SOLO levels and the type of data provided: irrelevant data, relevant data from a source, or "data and principles that are not given but which are relevant, hypothetical, and often implicit in the data" (Biggs & Collis, 1982, p. 28). Figure 4.1 provides a visual representation of the SOLO levels, each of which appears below the list of verbs associated with it.

As the name "structure of the observed learning outcome" implies, the SOLO taxonomy is intended to enable educators to evaluate students' levels of understanding through their responses. As you are reading the descriptions of each of the SOLO levels below, think about the four characteristics that are behind the progressive complexity of the levels and how these characteristics change from level to level: capacity (working memory needed), relating operation (connection between prompt and response), consistency and conclusion (learner's conflict between responding and consistency between the prompt and response), and structure (visual representation of data).

Figure 4.1   The SOLO Taxonomy

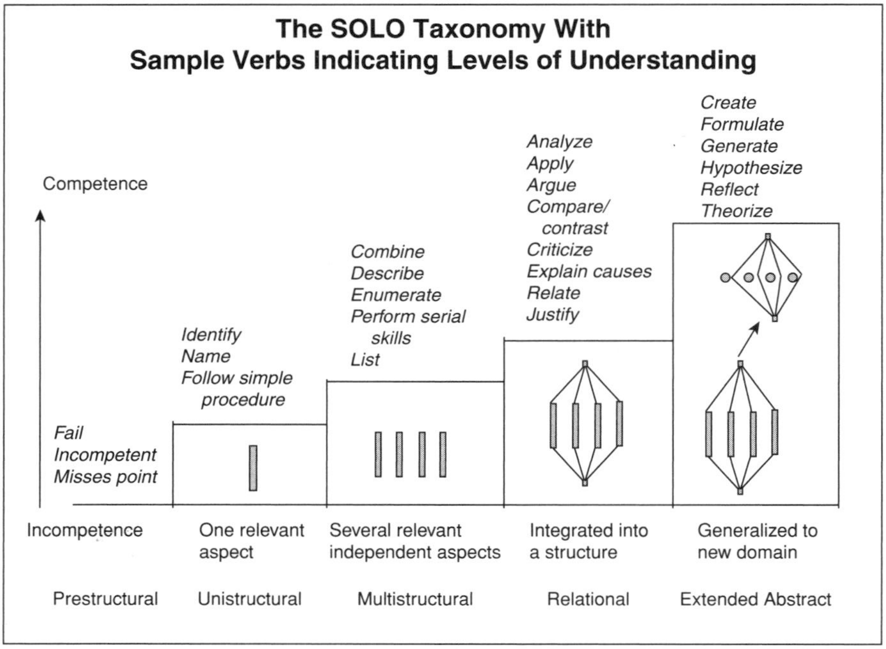

Source: Biggs (n.d.). Used with permission.

As you can see in Figure 4.1, prestructural responses are summarized as incompetent. A prestructural response, such as "I dunno," indicates a complete lack of understanding (or possibly lack of interest). As we progress in complexity, the unistructural student response represents a single idea or piece of information, hence the visual representation of one rectangle symbolizing an idea or piece of data. An example of a student response reflecting the unistructural level is "One of the oceans is the Atlantic Ocean." At the next SOLO level, multistructural, as the prefix indicates, student responses contain many ideas or pieces of information. A response at this level would be "The five oceans are the Atlantic Ocean, Pacific Ocean, Indian Ocean, Arctic Ocean, and Antarctic Ocean."

The important thing to remember about the multistructural level is that at this level no connections are drawn between the multiple ideas or pieces of information. As the example shows, a multistructural response is just a list. The ideas or pieces of information are all part of one response, but they are independent from each other. Both unistructural and multistructural responses are considered to be indicative of surface-level knowledge. As the complexity level increases to the relational and extended abstract levels, student responses are reflective of deeper levels of understanding that draw upon surface-level knowledge. Responses at the relational level, as the name implies, demonstrate relationships, or connections, between ideas or pieces of information. As the levels of responses increase in complexity, the demand on the student's working memory increases as well. This is an important concept to understand, as students will reach their cognitive load at different points based on their prior knowledge and ability to process new information. Continuing with the ocean example, a relational student response based on surface learning could be "The Pacific Ocean covers almost 46% of the Earth's surface, as compared to the Indian Ocean, which covers only 20% of the Earth's surface. The Pacific Ocean is double the size of the Indian Ocean."

At the most complex SOLO level, the extended abstract level, the student uses ideas and pieces of information not only to relate and make connections among them but also to extend them. In extended abstract responses, students "think beyond the given and bring in related, prior, or new knowledge, ideas, or information in order to create an answer, prediction, or hypothesis that extends to a wider range of situations" (Hattie, 2009, p. 29). A student response at the extended abstract level might sound like this: "Most likely the percentage of Earth's surface covered by oceans will only increase as glaciers continue to melt as a result of global warming, and the salt levels in the ocean could decrease, which might impact the fish who live in saltwater. Water is out of balance in the world; water makes the world go around, but it could also stop the world." Students responding at this level use surface and deep learning in conjunction with prior knowledge to make predictions and hypotheses. At this point they are beginning to engage in conceptual understanding. It is when students use their surface-level understanding in conjunction with their deep understanding to transfer their learning to new situations that they are experiencing conceptual understanding (Hattie, 2012).

You will notice in Figure 4.1 that particular verbs are associated with each of the levels of the SOLO taxonomy, with the exception of the prestructural level. The verbs in the figure do not constitute a comprehensive list—others can potentially be incorporated, as long as they are roughly synonymous with those listed. For example, at the unistructural level *state, define, recall,* and *tell* come to mind as additional verbs associated with one idea or piece of information. Actually, the list of SOLO learning verbs has been revised a bit in

Table 4.1   National Certificate of Educational Achievement Task Descriptors

SOLO Level	Unistructural	Multistructural	Relational	Extended Abstract
Additional verbs	Define, draw, find, label, match	Outline, follow an algorithm	Sequence, classify, explain effects, form an analogy, organize, distinguish, interview, question	Design, generalize, predict, evaluate, prove, plan, justify, argue, compose, prioritize, construct, perform

Source: Hook and Mills (2011, loc. 182 of 608).

New Zealand based on the National Certificate of Educational Achievement (NCEA) task descriptors list. Table 4.1 includes the additional words at each SOLO level on the NCEA task descriptor list that are not in the original SOLO taxonomy. Also note that a few words at the relational level on the SOLO taxonomy are in the extended abstract column on the NCEA word list (Hook & Mills, 2011). The beauty of a limited list of verbs in the taxonomy is that it simplifies the planning process while retaining the powerful attribute of increasing complexity. Why complicate the process with numerous verbs when what needs to be accomplished can be done with a simple limited list?

SOLO in Action

A handful of educational practitioners have been strong proponents of the power of the SOLO taxonomy, including New Zealand high school science teacher Steve Martin and Pam Hook, an educational consultant in New Zealand who has authored several books on the taxonomy and provides professional development to schools interested in it. A number of educational practitioners in England and Denmark have also adopted SOLO as their taxonomy of choice. In the United States, B. R. Jones (2014) has developed the focus model, which includes four practices that form the core of systematic school improvement: learning intentions, success criteria, formative assessment, and professional learning communities. All four of these practices are tightly aligned with the SOLO taxonomy, and in his discussion of learning intentions and success criteria Jones advocates the use of the SOLO taxonomy rather than Bloom's taxonomy or Webb's DOK.

I was first introduced to the SOLO taxonomy during my training to be a visible learning consultant for Corwin, and I've been a believer ever since. However, as a result of my extensive research in writing this book, reading about Martin's firsthand experience with the SOLO taxonomy and about how Hook has helped numerous teachers and schools in a number of countries establish a common language of learning through their use of the taxonomy, I have become not only a believer but also a staunch promoter of the taxonomy. Here is a summary of Martin's story, which is very enlightening.

SOLO in the Classroom

Steve Martin credits the SOLO taxonomy with renewing his passion for teaching high school science and with improving the effectiveness of student learning. He is devoted to SOLO when planning his high school science units, and his students have had tremendous success on New Zealand's national assessment. In addition, Martin has received several honors as a teacher, including New Zealand's top science teaching award in 2010. His unit design process using the SOLO taxonomy is elaborated in his book *Using SOLO as a Framework for Teaching* (2011). I highly recommend this book for content-area high school teachers interested in utilizing SOLO, as the taxonomy can be applied to *any* content area.

Up this point, my discussion of SOLO has focused on its use in determining the level of students' understanding based on their responses about what they have learned. However, as Martin (2011) eloquently states, the SOLO taxonomy "provides a simple, clear, and logical framework for a whole range of purposes including: learning intentions, success criteria, differentiation, self-assessment, peer assessment, goal setting, measuring progress, motivation, formative assessment, and questioning" (loc. 118–120 of 984). That is a powerful claim, but the taxonomy can back it up in regard to each of those purposes. I view performance tasks as part of the formative assessment process, or they can be part of summative assessment, which most likely would require questions to prompt the products or performances. In the classroom, the SOLO taxonomy is a one-stop supertool for planning, instruction, and assessment. Sign me up!

Martin's unit development model is broken down into three phases. It starts with a "generalized learning intention," which would equate to content-area standards. In the first phase, the facts, ideas, and concepts associated with the topic or unit being instructed are identified. This is similar to the KUD process, except that "understandings" are not identified in Martin's model. The facts, ideas, and concepts are then categorized into the four levels of understanding in the SOLO taxonomy: unistructural, multistructural, relational, and extended abstract. Martin's model actually combines the unistructural and multistructural levels at the high school level, since both represent surface-level learning. Essentially, the model identifies the "enabling knowledge" and knowledge that students need to know for that unit of study. In the second phase of Martin's unit development, the facts, ideas, and concepts that are grouped together at each of the SOLO levels are assigned SOLO verbs. The verbs selected are based on the learning outcomes the teacher wants to see. Phases 1 and 2 are the start of the learning progression. In the third and final phase, the SOLO verbs are combined with the pieces of knowledge that have been grouped with those verbs to create learning intentions and accompanying success criteria. Once the learning intentions and success criteria are written, a learning progression is complete, because as students move from the surface-level learning intentions of uni- and multistructural to the deep levels of understanding of relational and extended abstract, the level of complexity increases. Even though his process does not specifically identify "understandings" as in the KUD process, students are stretched and pushed to deep learning through the relational and extended abstract learning intentions and success criteria. This is where those essential understandings are formed.

Another practice that Martin incorporates into his classroom is the use of learning logs by students. Recall that the first component of writing learning intentions and success criteria is challenge. Writing learning intentions and success criteria at the four levels of understanding "provides a progression in the complexity of challenge to all students in the classroom"; as a result, there are most likely challenges appropriate for students at all levels of learning and progress, which also maintains "their engagement in what is being taught" (Martin, 2011, loc. 420 of 984) as well as their commitment to the learning. The learning log is the ultimate tool for differentiation, allowing for "differentiation in pace, prior knowledge, the demonstration of student knowledge, and the level of challenge" (loc. 518 of 984). Learning logs give students the ability to self-regulate their learning, no matter where their starting point is based on their prior knowledge. The surface level of learning at the unistructural and multistructural levels is an opportunity for all students to experience success, which drives student confidence. Additionally, the surface level of learning is a necessary part of the progression to the relational and extended abstract levels. When students who lack confidence in their ability to learn are successful with the surface level of learning, they may be encouraged to try the relational learning intentions and success criteria. With the right amount of scaffolding and feedback, such students can be successful.

Students maintain their own learning logs, so they are aware of all the learning intentions and success criteria for the unit of study. Learning logs, which serve as a means of making learning intentions and success criteria transparent, provide several learning opportunities, allowing students to

1. set their own goals;

2. make predictions on their success;

3. select appropriate learning strategies to support attainment of the success criteria;

4. self-assess their progress against the success criteria and make adjustments as needed; and

5. self-regulate their learning by answering the three big questions: "Where am I going?"; "How am I going?"; and "Where to next?"

Learning logs are the ultimate vehicle to support the development of assessment-capable learners. They have the potential to change both your teaching and student learning. Figure 4.2 provides an example of a student learning log that you can modify for your classroom.

Figure 4.2　Student Learning Log Sample

Student Learning Log

Name: Gretchen Silver

Unit of Study: Narrative and Opinion Writing

RL.3.3　Describe characters in a story (e.g., their traits, motivations, or feelings) and explain how their actions contribute to the sequence of events.

Student-friendly learning intention: You are learning to . . . describe characters in a story and explain how what they do affects the story line.

(Continued)

Figure 4.2 (Continued)

Learning Intention Level/Success Criteria		Student Learning Goal
Unistructural success criteria	Define what a character trait is.	I want to better understand what I am reading. I fall behind because I often have to re-read.
Unistructural success criteria	Define what character motivation is.	
Multistructural success criteria	Describe three characters.	
Relational success criteria	Explain a character's actions and how his/her actions lead to the order of events.	Learning Tactics
Extended abstract success criteria	Predict how the story would have changed if a character failed to take a critical action in the story.	I'm going to use the new "click or clunk" strategy Mr. Simpson taught us.
Learning Reflection		
When I read the first chapter, I read it paragraph by paragraph and I used Click or Clunk on each paragraph. There were a few times I needed to re-read a paragraph, but I was able to keep up with our book club, because I was checking for my understanding as I read rather than at the end of the reading. That felt good, because I could join in the conversations instead of having to re-read and miss out. Our book club discussed character traits and character motivation and came up with common definitions. I feel confident I've met the unistructural success criteria. We discussed all the characters. I added to the character descriptions of Mr. Arable, Wilbur, and Templeton. The relational success criteria was harder for me. Mr. Simpson had us write a response to a prompt, after we talked about it with our book club. We talked about Charlotte's actions and how her actions led to the others. I think my written response was okay. Mr. Simpson said I needed to be more specific in describing Charlotte's actions.		

Source: Hook and Mills (2011). Loc. 182 of 608

The SOLO taxonomy has begun making inroads in the United States. Michelle Caulk and Emily Peterson, the two teachers at W. Reily Brown Elementary School in Delaware mentioned in Chapter 2, used the SOLO taxonomy as they created their performance task. In reflecting on this experience later, Emily noted that using the taxonomy was difficult at first, but she also realized that it challenged her thinking on her instruction planning for her students. She observed that one issue she faced "was identifying the best SOLO verbs for each of the stages of the unit," because "each learning progression needed an appropriate SOLO verb at specific points in the students' learning." She went on to discuss the power of collaboration in the process: "I do think that reflecting and collaborating with other educators was meaningful during this point of the unit creation because oftentimes (myself guilty as well) educators feel most comfortable with, or refer to, lower-level learning activities and questioning. The SOLO verbs had made the unit stronger, as far as asking the students to build off of their prior knowledge, during each learning progression to dig deeper in their understanding." She mentioned also that she has been "incorporating several of the SOLO verbs into other subject areas." It is clear that Emily is well on her way to using the SOLO taxonomy for her instructional planning in order to challenge students and deepen their learning and understanding.

Be the Steve Martin of the United States

Here is your challenge! Share your story of using the SOLO taxonomy in your classroom. Be sure to include the connection between the taxonomy and the performance task(s) that you developed for your unit. In your submission, include your contact information in case there is a need to obtain releases for using your story on the performance task website or in a future publication. Submit your SOLO taxonomy story via email to performancetaskdesign@gmail.com, with "SOLO taxonomy submission" noted in the subject line.

SOLO in the School

Steve Martin's story is based on his work as a high school science teacher, but SOLO can become pervasive throughout all content areas and grade levels. Pam Hook and Julie Mills's book *SOLO Taxonomy: A Guide for Schools,* book 1, *A Common Language of Learning* (2011) is the first of a two-part series designed to support schools in their implementation of the SOLO taxonomy. Implementation has been the nemesis of many initiatives in schools and districts across the country, as too much effort is spent on the "what" and little time is spent on the "how" (Barber, Rodriguez, & Artis, 2016). Implementation of any new process can be daunting, so one of Hook and Mill's key focuses in the first book is to establish a common language of learning. Consistency in implementation relies on the existence of a common language, and in this case the language must be common not only among the educators in the building but among all the students as well.

A common language related to the SOLO taxonomy can go one step further in schools, using visual representations such as those in

Figure 4.1 and hand signals to reflect the different levels (Hook & Mills, 2011). Instead of a thumbs-up or thumbs-down to check for understanding, imagine this. A seventh-grade life sciences teacher is addressing the surface-level learning intentions for the various components of the process of digestion. She stops after every few components and checks for understanding by saying to the students, "Show me your level of SOLO understanding." At this point she should see students' hands displaying agreed-upon gestures, such as a single finger representing unistructural understanding or three fingers representing multistructural understanding (especially if she checked after presenting the three components of the process). It is possible that a few students may use their prior knowledge and display clasped hands in front of their bodies to represent relational understanding, because they are making connections between the mechanical breakdown of food (chewing) and the chemical job of amylase (in breaking down the food). Unless any students in the class have parents who are biology teachers, no students should be displaying their hands intertwined or clasped above their heads, the gesture representing an extended level of understanding. Students showing closed fists in front of them are indicating that they are at a prestructural level of understanding; they have completely missed the understanding of the knowledge and concepts presented by the teacher. There are many opportunities for good communication when a shared language of learning exists in a school.

Hook and Mills (2011) discuss six actions that schools, teachers, and students can take to develop a common language for the SOLO taxonomy:

- Display the visual representation of each of the SOLO levels and share SOLO learning outcomes throughout the school.
- Adopt "a common language of learning verbs aligned to SOLO outcomes" (loc. 152 of 608).
- Use the SOLO verbs to align standards, learning intentions, learning experiences, and assessments (formative and summative).
- Design formative assessment tasks as a means of developing understanding of the learning intentions at the SOLO levels.
- Provide guidance to students in using learning logs to monitor and self-regulate their learning.
- Utilize "effective learning strategies for SOLO learning verbs (HOT SOLO maps) and success criteria in self-assessment rubrics (HOT SOLO map rubrics) for achieving identified learning outcomes across all learning areas" (loc. 161 of 608).

Moving to the SOLO taxonomy starts with establishing a common language. Performance tasks fit right into these actions to develop a common language, as they can serve as learning experiences, formative assessments, or summative assessments. Having a common language of learning is the overarching concept in the development of a visible learner. Developing an assessment-capable learner is just one of four components of visible learning, and it has the greatest impact on student achievement, with a 1.44 effect size (Visible Learning[plus], n.d.-a). When students are able to utilize metacognitive strategies, which have an effect size of 0.69, they grasp the concept that they are able to self-regulate their learning (Hattie, 2009, 2012). The use of feedback (seeking, giving, receiving, and acting on it) is another attribute of a visible learner. As previously stated, feedback has an effect size of 0.75, and through performance tasks students engage in self- and peer assessment as a means of seeking, giving, and receiving feedback to promote increased understanding. The fourth attribute of a visible learner is the demonstration of desirable learning dispositions. Essentially, these are the positive characteristics that students display in dealing with learning situations, such as persistence and cooperation (Visible Learning[plus], n.d.-a). What are the dispositions of "thinking and doing" you want the students in your school to demonstrate and make a part of the everyday vernacular in the school? A common language of learning can have a powerful impact on your school. Start with a common language for the SOLO taxonomy as you venture into the implementation of performance tasks.

Final Thoughts

The two examples above, one from the classroom and one from a school starting the process of school-wide implementation, are just the tip of the iceberg. It is time we have some stories of success with the SOLO taxonomy in the United States. It is a powerful taxonomy with multiple uses that go beyond both Bloom's taxonomy and Webb's DOK, and it is a simplified taxonomy, with limited numbers of verbs for each level of understanding.

The SOLO taxonomy, in conjunction with learning logs and a common learning language, has the power to transform education dramatically for students, teachers, administrators, and parents. The use of the SOLO taxonomy in classrooms can further the development of assessment-capable learners and contribute to the advancement of visible learning. Students will be able to answer the three big questions: "Where am I going?"; "How am I going?"; and "Where to next?" They will have the opportunity to self-regulate their learning by predicting which levels of learning intention they can achieve based on their prior knowledge, and they will be able to select the learning tactics they will use to meet the success criteria and self- or peer assess as they go through the learning process. Students will build their confidence in learning as well as their resilience, and then they will be more willing to try to stretch their learning to the next level of understanding.

Once SOLO learning intentions and success criteria are developed, the building of the base will be complete. The SOLO learning intentions, especially at the unistructural, multistructural, and relational levels, are generated from the learning progressions. Just as your spine needs to have good alignment for you to stand up straight and not have back, hip, or neck issues, the base to your instruction and assessment needs proper alignment. The only way the performance task can have good alignment is if the base is built well, and the SOLO learning intentions and success criteria are the driving force behind the performance task that you create. Many unit learning intentions can be learned through performance tasks, and success criteria can be demonstrated through the completion of performance tasks, no matter if they are formative or summative in nature.

The process of writing SOLO learning intentions and success criteria is described below. Two examples are provided to support your learning.

Building the Base Step 3: Writing SOLO Learning Intentions and Success Criteria

At this point you have a few primary standards that you have selected for your unit, and you have created a learning progression, or multiple learning progressions, for each standard. In this final step of building the base, you will now use your learning progressions to write the learning intentions and success criteria for each of the standards. Just as a side note, if learning progressions have been established for each of the standards in your content area, you could pick and choose those standards that go together in a unit of instruction and save yourself time. Sometimes time put in up front saves time in the long run.

1. Reference your learning progressions, in addition to whatever tool you originally used to outline what it is that students need to know, understand, and do. It could have been a KUD, an "unwrapping" process, or some other process. When I followed the process I focused on the learning progressions.

Note that writing the learning progressions utilizing the SOLO verbs allows for an easier transition, as you are combining the "subskill" with the "enabling knowledge." Also note that it is very possible you may create more than one success criterion for a given learning intention at a particular level.

2. Start with writing the unistructural level and work your way up the hierarchical progression to the extended abstract level of understanding. Read a learning progression segment and identify the SOLO verb that aligns with what students need to know or be able to do in the learning progression. Write the success criteria for the learning intention. Follow this process for each of the learning progressions. If you do not have success criteria at certain levels of the SOLO taxonomy, you will need to write those criteria (in most cases this will be at the extended abstract level). It is possible that for high school students you may combine the unistructural and multistructural levels. The learning progressions you have written most likely are focused on the unistructural and multistructural levels and possibly the relational levels. It is very doubtful that your learning progressions include the deeper levels of understanding, especially extended abstract, as the progressions focus on the subskills and enabling knowledge, not on extending the knowledge and skills.

3. For each standard you should have SOLO learning intentions at each of the four levels. At the high school level, one column may represent both the unistructural and multistructural levels, but there should be a separate column for the relational learning intentions and another for the extended abstract learning intentions. So, for instance, in the secondary social studies example (Figure 4.4), just one portion of the standard is displayed (CE.2 has parts a–d). Each part would have its own SOLO learning intentions.

As you are creating your SOLO learning intentions, you may want to have at hand the lists of verbs for each level, both Biggs and Collis's list (see Figure 4.1), and the additional list of verbs approved for New Zealand's NCEA (see Table 4.1). (A comprehensive list of all these verbs is provided following the unit planning examples in Appendix 3.) Once you have developed your SOLO learning intentions and success criteria, the base for your performance task is complete, and you are ready to design and develop your performance task.

Two examples of learning progressions transitioned to SOLO learning intentions and success criteria are provided here: one from a grade 3 English language arts unit (Figure 4.3) and one from a grade 11 course in government (Figure 4.4). Each shows one of the learning progressions for one of the standards in the unit followed by the SOLO learning intentions and success criteria for the unit of study. Explanations and comments are noted in the margins. Take special note that there is not a learning intention present at each level because it would have been almost the same wording as the success criteria at that level. For instance, the learning intention would state "Define the five fundamental principles of government" and the success criteria would be "Define the five fundamental principles of government." Thus, there is no reason to repeat it. Understand that this may not always be the case. If the learning intention is "Identify organizational patterns when reading," the success criteria would most likely be "You are successful when you are able to identify cause/effect, problem/solution, chronological, and compare/contrast organizational patterns when reading."

Figure 4.3   Grade 3 Learning Progression Transitioned to SOLO Learning Intentions and Success Criteria

Grade 3 Unit

RL.3.2 Recount stories, including fables, folktales, and myths from diverse cultures; determine the central message, lesson, or moral and explain how it is conveyed through key details in the text.

		Subskills and Skills	Enabling Knowledge (information, facts) and Concepts
Learning Progression		Differentiate	Relevant and irrelevant details
		Identify	The central message
		Identify	Relevant details in relation to the central message
		Determine	Time order of key events
		Recount (retell)	Story
Understandings: "This is important to learn because . . ."		Stories are written to communicate key messages.	
		Authors include details to clearly communicate their key messages.	
		Stories are written with a key message and several supporting messages.	

As you are thinking about what you actually teach students for the learning progression, these two columns become the K and the D of KUD (know, understand, do). So there is no need to do these separately.

Students arrive at their own understandings, but it is necessary for teachers to think of possible key messages.

SOLO Level	Unistructural: One Idea	Multistructural: Many Ideas; No Connections Between Facts and Ideas	Relational: Connections Between Facts and Ideas	Extended Abstract: Generalize Learning and Apply to Different Contexts
Student-friendly learning intention: "We are learning to . . ."	Retell stories from different cultures and be able to state the central messages of the stories, along with details from the stories that support the messages. *Note, the full standard is the learning intention for the SOLO taxonomy. You will notice in the high school example, the full standard is broken down into a–d subcomponents. Each of those becomes a learning intention.*			
SOLO Verbs	Identify	List	Explain	Evaluate
Success criteria: "We are successful when we are able to . . ."	Identify a central message in a story.	List relevant details from a story that support the central message. List events in a story in order.	Explain how the relevant details convey the central message. Compare relevant to irrelevant details.	Evaluate which relevant detail was the most important in conveying the central message of the story.
Context for learning: "Students will engage in their learning by . . ."	*The context for learning will be completed in Step 4: Developing and Designing Performance Tasks.*			

Figure 4.4 Grade 11 Learning Progression Transitioned to SOLO Learning Intentions and Success Criteria

Grade 11 Unit: Virginia and U.S. Government

Learning Progression

CE.2 The student will apply social science skills to understand the foundations of American constitutional government by

a. explaining the fundamental principles of consent of the governed, limited government, rule of law, democracy, and representative government;

This is an example of one learning progression and its accompanying SOLO taxonomy. Note, the a) portion is the learning intention, as a–d are what students need to learn to understand the foundations of American government.

	Subskills and Skills	*Enabling Knowledge (information, facts) and Concepts*
Learning Progression	Define/describe	Consent of the governed
	Define/describe	Limited government
	Define/describe	Rule of law
	Formatively Check for Understanding	
	Define/describe	Representative government
	Define/describe	Democracy
Understandings: "This is important to learn because . . ."	American constitutional government is based on fundamental political principles that go back over two centuries.	
	These fundamental principles are present in our daily lives as U.S. citizens.	

	Unistructural: One Idea		*Extended Abstract: Generalize Learning and Apply to Different Contexts*
		Relational: Connections Between Facts and Ideas	
SOLO Level	*Multistructural: Many Ideas; No Connections Between Facts and Ideas*		
Student-friendly learning intention: "We are learning to . . ."	Explain the fundamental principles of American constitutional government.		

SOLO Verbs	Define/describe	Analyze	Predict
Success criteria: "We are successful when we are able to . . ."	Define each of the five fundamental principles of U.S. government (consent of the governed, limited government, rule of law, democracy, and representative government).	Analyze the significance of the principles of government and their importance to today's government.	Predict how the American government would change if one of the principles did not exist.
	Describe each of the five fundamental principles of U.S. government (consent of the governed, limited government, rule of law, democracy, and representative government).		
Context for learning: "Students will engage in their learning by . . ."		The context for learning will be completed in Step 4: Developing and Designing Performance Tasks.	

These two examples show two different standards and how they would transfer from learning progressions to SOLO learning intentions and success criteria. The learning context will be determined in Step 4, developing and designing performance tasks (see Chapter 5). Your base is now fully developed; it moves students from the surface level of learning to a deep level of learning. The SOLO taxonomy purposefully guides teachers to develop learning intentions and success criteria from the surface level to deeper levels of learning, which are often overlooked.

Follow Along: Creating a Performance Task

Step 3, writing SOLO learning intentions and success criteria, is a critical component as you design and develop your performance task to focus on the deeper levels of learning. If you are following along and creating your own performance task, it is now time to revisit the template.

1. Locate Step 3, "write SOLO learning intentions and success criteria." How your primary standards are written will determine what you place in the "Student-friendly learning intention: 'We are learning to . . .'" section of the template. If the primary standard does not have subcomponents (a–d) listed,

such as in the grade 3 example (Figure 4.3), you would rewrite the standard in student-friendly language in the "We are learning to" portion of the template. If your primary standard has subcomponents (a–d), then you will most likely be placing the subcomponents in student-friendly language in the learning intention portion of the template, as in the grade 11 social studies example (Figure 4.4).

2. Next, using Biggs and Collis's SOLO verbs and the additional National Certificate of Educational Achievement SOLO verbs in conjunction with your learning progressions, identify the SOLO verb that corresponds with the learning progression you are reading. Write that SOLO verb in the level of understanding to which it corresponds on the template in Step 3. Then write the SOLO success criteria for that particular learning progression segment. Your learning progression most likely will not take you past the relational level of understanding, and at that point it is necessary to stretch students' learning and understanding to the extended abstract level and create success criteria to do just that. You may have two or three unistructural and multistructural success criteria, or even more, depending on the grade level. The same is true at the relational and extended abstract levels as you increase in grade level. Feel free to split the boxes to add more cells to the column. Once you have your success criteria written at each of the levels of understanding, the base for your performance task is complete.

Key Takeaways

- Writing learning intentions and success criteria using the SOLO taxonomy provides further clarity to student learning.
- Learning intentions and success criteria need to be joined at the hip. One is no good without the other.
- Learning intentions and success criteria need to communicate clearly to students, so they can respond to the three big questions: "Where am I going?"; "How am I going?"; and "Where to next?"
- Learning intentions and success criteria need to take five elements into consideration: challenge, commitment, confidence, student expectations, and conceptual understanding.
- John Biggs and Kevin Collis designed the SOLO taxonomy as a tool for observing and measuring the quality of student understanding.

- There are five levels of understanding to the SOLO taxonomy: prestructural, unistructural, multistructural, relational, and extended abstract.
- The unistructural and multistructural levels are surface levels of understanding; the relational and extended abstract levels are deep levels of understanding.
- The SOLO levels progressively increase in capacity, relating operations, consistency and closure, and structure.
- Steve Martin of New Zealand has shared his story of using SOLO in his high school science classroom and how it revitalized him and his teaching, resulting in huge benefits for his students.
- Pam Hook, an educational consultant and author in New Zealand, supports school-wide implementation of SOLO from the primary level onward, starting with the development of a common language of learning.
- With wider use and greater exposure to its power for learning, the SOLO taxonomy has the potential to enhance student learning in the United States and close the achievement gap.
- The use of learning logs with SOLO has many benefits, including the development of assessment-capable learners.

Reflection Questions

1. What is the extent of the communication of learning intentions (goals, objectives) and success criteria in your classroom, or by your teachers? Where are improvements necessary?

2. What have you noticed about the effect sizes of the instructional practices that are associated with the development and implementation of performance tasks?

3. What is your reaction to the SOLO taxonomy? What do you see as the benefits of its use? Challenges?

4. What levels of understanding do your classroom questions and assessment questions target?

5. How do you see learning logs being used in your classroom?

6. What resonated with you the most in this chapter and why?

5

Performance Task Attributes

The base has been completed, and it is time to think about planning for instruction and assessment. If you are following along to create your own performance task as you are reading, you should have learning intentions and success criteria at each of the four SOLO levels of understanding as a result of the final step in building the base. The surface-level learning intentions and success criteria are most likely based on the subskills and enabling knowledge from the learning progressions that you developed in Step 2 of building the base. The deep levels of learning, relational and/or extended abstract learning intentions and success criteria, were probably developed based on the learning progression and understandings established through a KUD or other process. The deeper levels of understanding (relational and extended abstract) are intended to stretch student learning to the conceptual understanding level. You now have a crystal-clear picture of what the students need to learn. So what's next? It is time to plan your performance task. As noted previously, although performance tasks can serve as instructional learning experiences, formative assessments, or summative assessments, I prefer to use them as learning experiences.

Instructional learning experiences, formative assessments, and summative assessments all need to be aligned with the base that has been built, hence the importance of building a solid base. You will need to make a number of decisions in the process of determining

learning experiences and formative and summative assessments and
what each of those might entail. Before we dive into the creation of
the performance task, we need to take into consideration several attributes that contribute to the power of a performance task: alignment
with the SOLO learning intentions and success criteria; application of
knowledge, skills, and understandings; level of authenticity; level of
challenge; integration of 21st century skills; and scoring guides. If all
of these components are present, the result will be a powerful performance task.

Performance Task Attributes

Alignment With the SOLO Learning Intentions and Success Criteria

First and foremost, performance tasks are about students acquir-
ing the knowledge, skills, and understandings of the learning intentions so they can meet the success criteria. The learning intentions
and success criteria are the driving force behind the performance task
that is created, and as long as a solid base has been developed, there
will be alignment. Depending on how the performance task is used—
learning experience, formative assessment, or summative assessment—it is very possible that it will incorporate the learning of a few
learning intentions and demonstrate the attainment of several of the
success criteria. The critical factor is that the performance task developed needs to be aligned with the SOLO levels of the learning intentions and success criteria that were developed in the base.

Since a unit of study may have three or four primary focus standards, by the time you are finished constructing the base you could
potentially have between 12 and 25 success criteria. You are not going
to develop a performance task for each learning intention/success
criterion, so it may be appropriate to focus on the deep levels of relational and extended abstract when thinking of the performance task.
The surface levels of understanding are needed to move to the deeper
levels of understanding, where the surface levels of understanding
are applied. The SOLO taxonomy is designed to ensure that students
have the knowledge they need (uni- and multistructural levels of
understanding) before moving to the relational and extended abstract
levels. You need to know something before you can think more
deeply about it. This alignment with the learning intentions and success criteria requires students first to acquire knowledge and/or skills

at the surface levels before they can relate and extend the knowledge and skills. You do not want to dwell here, however, as students may lose their motivation if they spend too much time on surface-level understanding and the challenge becomes too easy. Interestingly, students are also likely to lose motivation if they are not given enough time to obtain a solid surface level of understanding, because then they are unable to make connections or extend their shaky knowledge from the surface level. Students need a stable surface level of understanding so they can access that knowledge readily for their next level of learning. As Hattie (2012) notes, "Together, surface and deep understanding lead to the student developing conceptual understanding" (p. 54). A balance of surface and deep understanding is needed to trigger students' development of conceptual understanding.

Application of Knowledge, Skills, and Understandings

This attribute might seem too obvious to include, considering we are discussing performance tasks, which essentially require students to "do" something, but it goes beyond just "doing." Application in a performance task is different from application of knowledge and skills on a worksheet. The difference lies in the fact that in a performance task the application of knowledge, skills, and understandings takes place within a context or novel situation (Martin-Kniep, 2011; McTighe, 2015). Consider the following learning context, used for the application of mathematics knowledge, skills, and understandings. The knowledge students will be applying will most likely include numerator, denominator, mixed fractions, and lowest common denominator. Possible skills are adding like and unlike fractions, dividing fractions, and simplifying fractions. A possible understanding might be, "The use of fractions applies to everyday activities."

You are an aspiring baker and want to appear on the Food Network's program *Kids Baking Championship*. You are practicing making large batches of salted-caramel chocolate cupcakes. Your current recipe makes 18 cupcakes, and you want to make a total of 27 cupcakes. Use your current recipe to create a new recipe with ingredient amounts for 27 cupcakes. Remember, when it comes to baking, exact measurements are of critical importance!

This is where the four levels of the SOLO taxonomy can lend a helping hand. When it comes to application, you have to apply knowledge, skills, and understandings. You first have to know something and do something before you can apply it to a unique situation. This is where surface-level learning and unistructural and multistructural learning intentions and success criteria come into play. Since students need knowledge and skills before they can apply them, it only makes sense that they apply them at the relational and extended abstract levels to stretch their learning and conceptual understanding. The critical factor to remember is that the performance task, no matter where it falls on the continuum, needs to meet the demands of the success criteria at the level of understanding intended. If the learning intentions and success criteria are written at the relational level, then the component of the performance in which students will show evidence of learning truly needs to be relating ideas and/or information learned at the surface level. The application of knowledge, skills, and understandings is closely connected to the next attribute of level of authenticity. The more authentic a performance task, the better; however, a task does not have to be real-time authentic, as discussed below.

Level of Authenticity

Recall the performance task continuum introduced in Chapter 1. The more authentic a performance task can be, the greater student motivation, because students can identify with the relevance of the task. Authentic tasks, which essentially are real-time problems or situations that students can tackle, are not readily available. However, teachers can create performance tasks that have a high level of authenticity by creating real-world situations incorporating real-world products and performances associated with real occupations and positions and delivered to real audiences.

There is no doubt that the more authentic a performance task, the more powerful it is. Merriam-Webster.com provides both "simple" and full definitions of the word *authentic*. The simple definition that applies to a performance task includes the descriptions "real and genuine" and "made to be or look just like the original." In the full

Figure 5.1 Performance Task Continuum

Basic Task   Real-World Task   Authentic Task

Student relevance, engagement, motivation

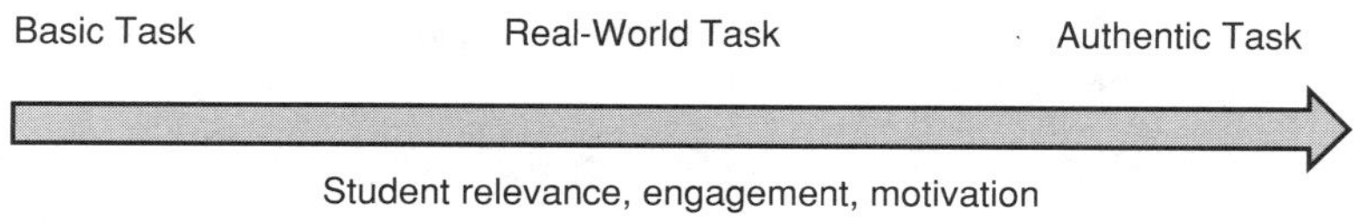

definition, the following fits the bill as well: "conforming to an original so as to reproduce essential features." Simply stated, the more authentic the performance task, the more successful it will be in promoting students' understanding as well as engagement and motivation. The attribute of authenticity is supported by numerous educational practitioners (Ainsworth, 2015; Cohen, 1995; Knight, 2013; Martin-Kniep, 2000, 2011; McTighe, 2015; Moon, Brighton, Callahan, & Robinson, 2005; Reeves, 2004), some of whom, including Martin-Kniep (2000, 2011) and Knight (2013), rely solely on the simple definition of authentic performance tasks as "real or genuine tasks." They promote authentic tasks that are "real and genuine" versus real-world tasks that are "made to be or look just like the original."

What determines the level of authenticity of a performance task? Two primary components bring authenticity to a performance task. First, a powerful performance task is a real-world task. The task itself needs to be a product or performance that a person would do as part of an occupation or career. That is, the task, as well as the profession or career in which someone would complete the task, should be representative of the real world. If a performance task addresses an actual current problem in the school or community that is appropriate for the curriculum, that adds another level of authenticity, but you won't always be fortunate enough to have the opportunity to address such problems. Second, a powerful performance task has a real-world audience. When an accountant completes a tax return, the audience is the client; when a speechwriter writes a speech for the governor, the audience is not only the governor but also the people the governor will be addressing, such as the League of Women Voters. In each of these examples the performance task is "made to be or look just like the original." Each is a real-world task in that it is presented to someone. Other kinds of audiences for performance tasks might be managers or community organizations.

An authentic performance task may seek to solve a problem for the greater good of the school or community, or it may involve a product or performance that addresses students' own needs. If you have working high school students, for example, they could complete their own income tax forms. This would be a "genuine and real" performance task, but it may not be aligned with the learning intentions/success criteria. That might depend on the course of study the students are taking—there are accounting courses in high schools in which such a performance task just might be applicable. The point is, the more authentic the learning context, the more relevant the learning, which drives motivation and engagement.

Incorporating real-world tasks is a great way to expose students of all ages to different professions and careers and the types of products they create or performances they present. Additionally, such tasks offer opportunities for students to work in collaborative teams, just as many professionals do on a daily basis. In every profession or career it is necessary to be able to create products of some type or to perform in specific ways. A financial analyst, for example, communicates with clients verbally and in writing, analyzes clients' financial status, and helps clients plan for retirement by creating spreadsheets that display percentages of financial growth expected over numbers of years. A journalist for a magazine such as *The Economist* needs to have strong research skills, communication skills to interview people, and writing skills. For a Broadway actor, the ultimate performance takes place when the curtain goes up and the show starts. However, there is more to the actor's job, such as researching the character to be played; maybe taking lessons to perfect some element of the character, like a particular accent; and perhaps meeting with the choreographer to learn a sequence of dance steps for the production. A florist needs to be able to create beautiful flower arrangements but also must be able to determine the amount of flowers to order for a wedding and to estimate the cost of the arrangements accurately so that the florist's business makes a profit. A researcher at the Infectious Disease Research Institute in Seattle, Washington, may create products to diagnose diseases, conduct experiments to create vaccines, or plan treatment strategies. For all of these professions, there are audiences, or recipients of the products and performances: clients preparing for retirement; magazines' readership; Broadway audiences; a bride, a groom, and wedding party guests; ailing people across the globe. Linda Darling-Hammond (2008) encourages teachers to create *"ambitious and meaningful tasks* that reflect how knowledge is used in the field" (p. 5), and that is exactly what real-world performance tasks can do.

The performance task continuum reflects the importance of authenticity in relation to relevance. Imagine a high school biology class that is studying a unit on the environment. Students might evaluate how the school could reduce its environmental footprint, create an action plan, present it to the board of education or at public hearings at different sites, and implement the action plan if approved. Fifth-grade students could write short stories and read them to students in the primary grades and then provide copies of the stories for the students to take home. This may sound like a simple performance task, but it all comes down to the learning intentions and success criteria that are driving the learning. There are many benefits to this type of performance task, and they go beyond integrating reading, writing, listening, and speaking all in one task. Such tasks serve the greater good in the community and school. There is a purpose to the learning. One of the high-impact instructional strategies that Jim Knight details in his book *High-Impact Instruction: A Framework for Great Teaching* (2013) is authentic learning. He highlights several benefits, of which "purpose" is the first. His words on purpose are at the heart of being a teacher:

> More important, authentic learning at its best kindles a desire in students to learn more about fascinating and meaningful topics that they might otherwise not have known about—a crucial goal for education. By structuring learning experiences so that they are relevant and engaging by demonstrating how important it is to pursue a project with a meaningful mission, authentic learning can lead students to a deeper understanding of the power of purpose. (p. 228)

There is no doubt that the more authentic a performance task is, the more powerful it can be in enhancing student learning and students' desire to learn and be challenged. However, performance tasks at the extreme authentic end of the continuum are few and far between, as they require particular current situations in the school, the community, the state, or the world that relate to the learning standards.

Real-world performance tasks allow you to go wild with your creativity, and they still have a high level of authenticity. Remember, you should focus on the learning and not just on the performance task, which serves as a vehicle for the learning. When performance tasks are authentic, whether "real and genuine" or "made to be or look just like the original," they add relevance, engagement, and motivation to the learning (Ainsworth, 2010; Knight, 2013; Martin-Kniep, 2011). The importance of relevance is demonstrated in the reflections Michelle Caulk shared about the following performance task, which she and Emily Peterson created around Black History Month:

> **Performance Task—fourth grade:** In honor of Black History Month, the school principal would like your opinion of who should be honored in the school's display case. Write a letter to the principal telling her about an influential African American and why that person should be honored.

Michelle observed: "The students have completed a unit on opinion writing. This performance task served as evidence to their understanding of opinion writing. The students were highly engaged because this particular task presented a realistic scenario of their principal and school. It conveyed purpose and relevance to the students, helping them achieve a successful product." Michelle and Emily's completed performance task template, along with a few student opinion letters, appears in Appendix 1. Michelle and Emily were supported by their achievement liaison teacher, Monica McCurry, and their principal, Dr. Susan Frampton.

Relevance is critical especially at the middle and high school levels, when student engagement begins to wane. In the 2009 High School Survey of Student Engagement, 42% of students who had considered dropping out said that they had done so because they did not find the work they were doing relevant. They wanted their schoolwork to be related to what they might do later in their lives professionally (Yazzie-Mintz, 2010). This finding supports the idea that using performance tasks that are "made to be or look just like the original" is an acceptable way of making learning relevant. The 2009 data also revealed that 66% of high school students were bored in class every day, and 42% of respondents said that one of the reasons for their boredom was the lack of relevance of the materials being used (Yazzie-Mintz, 2009). A 2012 Gallup poll of 500,000 students asked about their engagement in school and found that as students progressed from elementary to middle school and then to high school, their level of learning engagement decreased. At the high school level only 4 out of every 10 students indicated they were engaged (Busteed, 2013). When students see the relevance and meaningfulness in what they are learning, their engagement and motivation increase.

Simply sharing with your high school science students that they will be conducting an experiment on conductivity and reporting the findings is not exactly the most motivating or engaging way to approach the task. This is where the motivating context comes into play and brings performance tasks to life.

Motivating Context

The motivating context increases the level of authenticity of the real-world performance task so that students become engaged in their learning. In their Understanding by Design model, Grant Wiggins and Jay McTighe (2005) use the acronym WHERETO in Stage 3, planning learning experiences. The acronym represents the entire planning process, but I want to focus here on the *H*—the "hook." The hook is intended to engage students throughout the learning experience. The motivating context does the same thing, not only capturing students' attention at the start of the learning experience but also carrying the motivation and engagement throughout the unit of study by involving a real audience. The purpose of the motivating context is limited to providing a level of authenticity to the performance task, yet through this context the learning becomes relevant, which in turn drives student engagement and motivation. When writing the motivating context, you should keep the success criteria in mind. There are three main components to the motivating context:

- Position, career, or occupation
- Product or performance of the position, career, or occupation
- Audience—recipient of the product or performance

Below are some examples of performance tasks with the motivating contexts noted. These examples do not include the directions students would receive in order to complete the performance tasks, and each displays only a couple of the standards to show the connections of the tasks to the standards.

Grade 2, English Language Arts: Example of a Performance Task, Short Planning Description

RI.2.1 Ask and answer such questions as *who, what, where, when, why,* and *how* to demonstrate understanding of key details in a text.
W.2.2 Write informative/explanatory texts in which they introduce a topic, use facts and definitions to develop points, and provide a concluding statement or section.

Occupation: Educational specialist for Monterey Bay Aquarium
Product or performance: Information flyer
Audience: Visitors to the aquarium

> I love the Internet. I selected these standards first, then came up with a role, product, and audience. I tried to tap into student likes at this age but did not want the typical zoo scenario. I did a search for aquarium jobs online and up came Monterey Bay Aquarium and staff members sharing their jobs. WOW! How easy was that!

Student Motivating Context

The Monterey Bay Aquarium is updating some of its exhibits with sea creatures that are new to the aquarium. The sea creatures arrive next week. There is not enough time to have the standard informational displays installed. You and your team have been charged with creating an information flyer on each of the new sea creatures.

> Remember to write at the students' reading level. This might need a little adjustment.

As I created the motivating context for the example above, my mind went into overdrive, thinking about a number of different topics. I was thinking that I needed to find resources at the students' reading levels, as what they read will be the driving force behind what they create. I recognized that not all components in the reading standard are applicable for this product, and I need to be very explicit in the student directions to ensure that the success criteria are incorporated.

Grade 7, CCSS Mathematics: Example of a Performance Task, Short Planning Description

7.RP Ratios and Proportions: Analyze proportional relationships and use them to solve real-world and mathematical problems.
7.NS The Number System: Apply and extend previous understandings of operations with fractions to add, subtract, multiply, and divide rational numbers.
Occupation: Financial analyst
Product or performance: Financial report (written component, spreadsheets)
Audience: Client—Ms. Farmer

Student Motivating Context

You are a financial planner for Merrill Lynch. You recently began working with a new client, Cybil Farmer, who is 57 years old, single, and employed as a professor in the Sociology Department at the University of Washington. She would like to retire at the age of 62, and she has provided you with the following documents:

1. Average yearly expenses, categorized
2. Salary and average yearly increases over the past three years
3. Goals for retirement
4. Present investments
5. Savings each month that are invested

Can Ms. Farmer comfortably retire at age 62 with a $10,000 cushion for unexpected expenses? Prepare an analysis of her financial status and create a report to present your findings and a proposed retirement plan.

This is a challenging real-world problem that applies all four operations. This is a task "made to be or look just like the original," but it brings relevance to the learning. As I think about this motivating context, I know I need to come up with categorized yearly expenses, a salary, retirement goal, and present investments and savings for each month. In order to add a twist to the performance task, I decide to place in a container slips of paper showing different amounts of present investments and amounts of savings, and ask each student to draw a slip from the container without looking. I had considered having students roll a die or deal playing cards a certain number of times to determine present investments and savings amounts, but then I thought, "What is the learning in having students do that? It would just be a waste of time."

Knowing students' interests helps in the creation of meaningful motivating contexts, and interests differ across developmental age levels (primary, elementary, middle school, and high school). For example, if you are studying mammals in a second-grade science class, it helps to know that most elementary students would love to be able to be zookeepers, or large-animal veterinarians. In such a case, it can be relatively easy to develop a performance task targeting the science learning intentions/success criteria. I once observed a kindergarten class in which each student created his or her own book on a sea creature based on research that was done through a shared learning experience. All the students had the opportunity to read their books to the class from the "author's chair." With primary students (K–2) you have a bit of leeway, due to their developmental stages, in respect to the level of authenticity of performance tasks. K–2 students believe in Santa Claus, the Tooth Fairy, and the Easter Bunny, so it's okay if the motivating context happens to be something like writing to a cartoon character or other fictional character, as long as real-world performance tasks are periodically interspersed. By the time students get to third grade, the shift from learning to read to reading to learn is in full force, and that is an opportune time to commit to real-world motivating contexts the majority of the time you implement performance tasks.

Integration of Two or More Subject Areas and 21st Century Skills

Performance tasks become powerful when students apply knowledge and skills from different subject areas within the tasks (Ainsworth, 2015; Martin-Kniep, 2011; McTighe, 2015). This is closely linked to the level of authenticity as well. In most occupations and professions, knowledge and skills from different domains are integrated with English language arts (reading, writing, listening and speaking, and language), across all positions. Performance tasks are often interdisciplinary, and the CCSS Literacy in History/Social Studies, Science, and Technical Subjects clarify the English language skills that are needed for content areas. The layout of the Next Generation Science Standards includes a section at the bottom of the page on each standard titled "Connections," which specifies how the standard connects to both the ELA and Math CCSS. The financial analyst from the seventh-grade mathematics motivating context needs to be able to use mathematical skills as well as English language arts skills of writing and verbal communications when presenting the financial plan to Ms. Farmer. Performance tasks, whether they are products, performances, or a combination of both, typically incorporate two or more subject areas, with English language arts the most common co-subject area. Even in the example of the journalist for *The Economist,* in which English language arts is the predominant subject area, the student will still need to employ research skills, which most likely would be around a topic related to the economy or government. Standards for the Broadway actor would most likely be from the arts as well as English language arts, with an emphasis on speaking and listening standards.

Embedded in all of the professions presented earlier in the chapter—financial analyst, journalist, Broadway actor, florist, research scientist—are 21st century skills, yet such skills are often overlooked in the classroom. The Partnership for 21st Century Learning (2015) organizes 21st century skills into a framework made up of four major components: key subjects and 21st century themes (global awareness; financial, economic, business, and entrepreneurial literacy; civic literacy; health literacy; environmental literacy); information, media, and technology skills (information literacy; media literacy; information, communications, and technology [ICT] literacy); learning and innovation skills (critical thinking and problem solving; creativity and innovation; communication and collaboration); and life and career skills (flexibility and adaptability; initiative and self-direction; social and cross-cultural skills; productivity and accountability; leadership and responsibility). In many

cases you will probably integrate a number of these skills into your performance tasks without recognizing that they are 21st century skills. You may need to familiarize yourself with others of these skills so that you can purposefully integrate them into your daily instructional plans. You can access resources for teaching 21st century skills at the website of the Partnership for 21st Century Learning (http://www.p21.org) or by scanning the QR code on page 106. It might be a good idea to keep the *P21 Framework Definitions* document handy to reference during instructional planning (Partnership for 21st Century Learning, 2015).

If you are struggling to think of professions and careers, try consulting one or both of the following sources to trigger some ideas. Each year, *U.S. News & World Report* produces a list of the 100 best jobs for that year (access at http://money.usnews.com/careers/best-jobs/rankings/the-100-best-jobs, or scan the QR code in the margin). The Guide to the World of Occupations is another good source; this site provides information on activities that different jobs entail along with a wealth of other information that may help you determine what products or performances your students could complete (access at http://www.occupationsguide.cz/en, or scan the QR code in the margin).

Level of Challenge

To design a performance task that is appropriately challenging, in many cases you will need to incorporate some flexibility to ensure that the task is neither too difficult nor too easy for students. Just as Goldilocks needed to find the "just right" porridge, students need to experience the "just right" amount of challenge. As mentioned in Chapter 4, it is interesting to note that teachers and students view challenge differently. Teachers see the performance task itself as being challenging or not, whereas students see their ability to complete the performance task or not as the challenge (Hattie, 2012). The SOLO taxonomy learning intentions and success criteria play a critical role in the development of a performance task, as the focus of the task is not merely completing the task itself but also engaging students in the "challenge of learning" (Hattie, 2012, p. 51). The goal is to plan instructional learning experiences, which may include performance tasks, that engage students, so they are committed to learning. This requires that the learning intentions and success criteria have just the right amount of challenge. As Hattie (2012) notes, "It is challenge that keeps us investing in pursuing goals and committed to achieving goals" (p. 51).

The SOLO taxonomy is useful in this situation, as students first learn and understand the surface-level knowledge (facts, ideas, and concepts) they need in order to relate and extend that knowledge to deeper levels. The performance task, or a series of performance tasks, can be constructed so that students are successful with the surface level of learning and then can be stretched to attempt the deep levels of learning in the next performance task. The key to determining the "just right" amount of challenge to engage students in learning is to tap into students' prior knowledge before instruction commences, because that prior knowledge can provide insights into what level of challenge will engage students rather than bore or frustrate them. Chapter 7 provides more detailed discussion of the role of prior knowledge in the planning of performance tasks.

Scoring Guide, aka Rubric

When it comes to a product or performance, a scoring guide, or rubric, is needed to measure how well the expected criteria have been met. If there is no scoring guide, the evaluation of the product or performance is subjective on the part of the teacher. The success criteria for the learning intentions form the cornerstone for the development of criteria for the scoring guide. The main difference between the success criteria and the scoring guide is that the scoring guide distinguishes levels of quality, whereas the success criteria constitute simply a checklist. There should be close alignment between the success criteria within the unit of instruction and the performance task scoring guides. Chapter 6 provides detailed information on the development of scoring guides for performance tasks, as well as the benefits of scoring guides.

Performance Task Decisions

You will need to make a few decisions when creating performance tasks that are aligned with your learning intentions and success criteria. The first decision concerns what product or performance will offer the best means of demonstrating the success criteria. (Appendix 4 presents a list of possible products and performances for your consideration—it is not a complete list, but it can serve as a starting point.) This first decision is closely related to the next: choosing which success criteria can be demonstrated through the product or performance you have selected. The final decision will be whether the performance task will be an instructional learning experience (and thus formative in nature), a culminating performance task that serves a summative purpose, or a combination of both.

Let me pause here to recognize that the word *assessment* has come to have a bad connotation. Assessment has become something to dread, like getting a letter from the IRS saying you're going to be audited. You just cringe at the thought. However, *formative assessment* and *summative assessment* are the terms commonly used in relation to the gathering of student evidence of learning. We are talking about performance tasks, and assessment is not part of the name, but both PARCC and SBAC, the consortia that created the high-stakes assessment systems currently used to measure student progress on the Common Core State Standards, have performance tasks as part of their assessments. Thus, these performance tasks are summative in nature—they measure what students have learned. Additionally, both the PARCC and SBAC assessment systems have formative assessment components that can be administered throughout the year if districts decide to use them. These interim assessments are intended to enable teachers to make instructional adjustments based on student progress. So, performance tasks can swing both ways: They can be formative or summative in nature, or a combination of both.

The key to determining if a performance task is formative or summative is how you use the evidence that students generate. If students are able to make revisions to the performance task, or you provide additional instruction to close the gap on student understanding as a result of the performance task, then it is being used formatively. A performance task that includes an oral presentation on a research topic resulting in a score that goes into a grade book would be considered summative. After reading that sentence, you may be thinking, "Is an oral presentation on a research project likely to stretch a student's thinking to deep understanding?" You need to remember that if the teacher has created the SOLO learning intentions and success criteria at the surface and deep levels, it is very possible that the oral presentation could focus on the success criteria for the relational and extended abstract; the content of the oral presentation is the focus of the learning, whereas the presentation is the vehicle (versus a written product). The only way we can know if the student's response is actually at the relational and extended abstract levels is to hear the presentation. Remember, you may develop relational and extended abstract learning intentions, but that does not mean that what the student produces is at the relational and extended abstract levels. SOLO was originally developed to measure the quality of student responses and to show that students' learning results demonstrate different levels of understanding to the same prompts.

Once the base is complete, the next step in instructional planning tends to be to determine how you will assess (formative and summative) students to gather evidence of how they are learning (formative) and what they have learned (summative). As much as performance tasks can be used formatively, this book is not about formative assessment. Just know that formative assessment comes in a number of different forms, from checking for understanding, quick progress checks, to full common formative assessment models with pre- and post-assessments that occur during the learning process. All of these have their place in the classroom—it is a matter of selecting the right tool to match the intended purpose.

Here is a closer look at each of the three main decisions that need to be made in the creation of a performance task.

Product or Performance

In choosing a product or performance, you have limited options. Products can take a few different forms. A product might be a physical item, such as a sculpture in an art class, a meal created in a home and careers class, or something written, such as a play script in English or an information guide in social studies. In some cases it is obvious that you need to have a task in which students write or speak responses to show evidence of their learning based on the standards themselves, in particular the writing, speaking, and listening standards. In others you have some leeway in making decisions as to how students will learn, if it is a learning experience, or demonstrate what they have learned, including the area of reading. The key is to remember that the product or performance should offer at least a minimally real-world level of authenticity while still challenging and stretching students' thinking and learning. The list of possible products and performances in Appendix 4 may be helpful in activating your thinking.

When it comes to determining whether your performance task will be a product or a performance, you need to let the standards themselves guide you in your decision-making process. The success criteria will play second fiddle to the standards in this decision. By demonstrating the success criteria, you attain the full standard; thus, it is essential to consider the standard first and the success criteria second. The important point to remember here is that the product or performance needs to be something that a real person would complete in a real-world job position, career, or occupation.

In the ELA CCSS it is clear that you will have students create a written product if there is a writing standard within your unit, such as an informational/explanatory text, argument, or narrative of some type. The same would be the case for the speaking standards—hence the importance of referencing the standards in deciding on a product or performance. The motivating context you create determines the specific product students will write based on the position, career, or occupation that produces that product and who the typical recipient of the product is. When it comes to the reading standards, as a result of how they are written, they could be incorporated into written or oral performance tasks.

Take a look at this third-grade reading standard:

RL.3.3 Describe characters in a story (e.g., their traits, motivations, or feelings) and explain how their actions contribute to the sequence of events.

I envision students reading books of their own choice and gathering in small literature groups of about four students each. After lessons on character traits, motivations, and feelings, students could have conversations in their groups describing the characters in the books they are reading and maybe sharing the plots of the books thus far. As each student orally shares, the others could be using the success criteria as they listen to their peers and then provide feedback. Another lesson could take place on character actions and their relation to the sequence of events, followed by another meeting of the literature groups that would follow the same process. In both of these instances students are basically in a "book club"—an idea that has become very prevalent over the past several years. Obviously, this could be further fleshed out as a performance task, but the point is that with this particular reading standard, students can learn to describe characters and explain how their actions affect the sequence of events through oral conversation in a "book club," or they could provide written descriptions and explanations, most likely on a traditional assessment.

Some standards just don't lend themselves to being incorporated into a performance task, and that's okay—we have other means to assess students' learning formatively and summatively, and to determine whether they have attained the success criteria. For instance, you might have your fourth-grade students create a collage or diorama to depict the most important event in *Tuck Everlasting,* by Natalie Babbitt, and then present it to the class. For such a task, you would be hard-pressed to find a position, career, or occupation—with the exception of artist—in which a diorama or collage is a typical product.

You want the learning, and not the product, to be the focus, and real-world products and performances are a means of keeping the focus on the learning rather than on the doing. There is no harm in creating a traditional pen-and-paper test with selected-response and short-response questions if certain success criteria do not lend themselves to the product or performance you have identified for your performance task. The intention of this book is to encourage you to incorporate more performance tasks, so that students are applying what they have learned at the different levels of understanding in real-world situations and contexts. Of course, there are a number of products and performances in real-life jobs, especially in preparation for jobs, that utilize pencil-and-paper or computer-administered assessments. Just think of your teacher licensing test or driver's license test. In most states, teacher licensing tests are traditional tests with selected-response, short-response, and extended-response questions. Depending on the state, you may also have to submit a video of yourself teaching a class. The driver's license test in most states is a traditional test, in combination with a performance task of driving. The beauty of the SOLO taxonomy learning intentions and success criteria is that they can be used to create any type of assessment, traditional or performance based, or questions to be asked in classroom discussions. The question you need to ask is, "What learning intentions/success criteria could be learned through the product or performance identified, or how could students demonstrate what they have learned through the product or performance?" This leads us to the second decision you need to make after you have chosen the product or performance that students will complete.

Success Criteria for the Performance Task

Once you have identified the product or performance students will complete based on the standards, you next need to focus on the SOLO learning intentions and success criteria you have written for the unit. As previously noted, the SOLO learning intentions and success criteria are purposefully written to progress in complexity from the unistructural to the extended abstract levels of understanding on each standard within the unit of study. The success criteria are representative of what students need to do in order to demonstrate their level of understanding of the learning intentions. In order for students to tackle the relational and extended abstract levels of understanding, they need to first have a strong understanding of the unistructural and multistructural levels.

SOLO relational and extended abstract levels lend themselves to performance tasks, as those learning intentions and success criteria focus on making connections between ideas and information and extending ideas and information. However, depending on the performance task, it is very possible that the surface-level success criteria can also be demonstrated through the performance task. You will need to evaluate each success criterion in the unit to determine which ones can be incorporated into the performance task you have selected. Focus on incorporating the relational and extended abstract levels into your performance task, but do not try to force them into the performance task. It is acceptable to have surface-level success criteria in the performance task if they fit.

Performance Task Model Options

The final decision you must make is whether the performance task will be a learning experience, a summative culminating performance task, or a combination of formative performance task and summative culminating performance task. First, you can simply create a summative performance task that is completed to determine if the success criteria have been met. Second, you could have a series of performance tasks that build the knowledge and skills that are representative of the four levels of success criteria.

The first option is to create a real-world performance task that serves as an instructional learning experience, meaning that students will be participating in parts of the performance task as instruction is occurring, and at the end of instruction the performance task will be complete. In *Common Formative Assessments 2.0,* Larry Ainsworth (2015) mentions performance tasks in connection to his CFA 2.0 model, but they are not an actual component of the CFA 2.0 model. Ainsworth notes that performance tasks "serve a critical purpose in helping students develop deep understanding of the learning intentions during the unit so students are better prepared to demonstrate all they have learned on the post-CFA at the end of the unit" (p. 47).

He describes performance tasks as "mini-culminating events" throughout a unit in which students are applying the concepts and skill they are learning. In this model, real-world performance tasks are used solely as learning experiences.

An important aspect to this is the fact that throughout the unit the students are applying concepts and skills they have learned, so they are first learning the concepts and skills (surface-level understanding) and then applying those concepts and skills through a real-world performance task. In this case the completion of performance task, at both the surface and deep levels, is part of the learning experience, and thus the performance task is formative in nature. The best way to describe this model is through an example.

Let's say you are teaching a seventh-grade English class and it is near the end of the first quarter. You recognize the importance of argument writing across the subject areas, in life, and on the high-stakes assessments. You are aware of what students should have learned through sixth grade, but you want your own evidence. You plan on providing students a writing prompt that you found on the *New York Times* Learning Network blog (see Gonchar, 2015) because you know that this site annually sponsors an editorial contest addressing an important issue. The blog provides a built-in audience through its online writing contests. From the blog you select one of the argument-writing prompts: "Do apps help you or just waste your time?" Since your seventh-grade class writes several arguments during the year, learning intentions and success criteria for writing arguments have been developed, as well as a standard scoring guide. You share the learning intentions, success criteria, and argument scoring guide with the students.

Figure 5.2   Writing Standard for Argument Writing

W.7.1 Write arguments to support claims with clear reasons and relevant evidence.

  a. Introduce claim(s), acknowledge alternate or opposing claims, and organize the reasons and evidence logically.

  b. Support claim(s) with logical reasoning and relevant evidence, using accurate, credible sources and demonstrating an understanding of the topic or text.

  c. Use words, phrases, and clauses to create cohesion and clarify the relationships among claim(s), reasons, and evidence.

  d. Establish and maintain a formal style.

  e. Provide a concluding statement or section that follows from and supports the argument presented.

You tell your students that this writing prompt is serving as a pre-assessment, so you can determine their learning needs. You establish with the class that there will be instructional components addressing common needs, identified from the writing pre-assessment, followed by time for them to revise their writing. As students are revising, you will be able to conference with individual students or small groups to address their needs. Based on the pre-assessment results, you are able to determine the daily learning intentions and success criteria that are based on the argument-writing standard as displayed in Figure 5.2. You provide two class periods for students to write their arguments, and they can do research at home as well. You provide all students with their scores on the pre-assessment scoring guide based on the arguments they have written in response to the prompt "Do apps help you or just waste your time?" and since they have the unit learning intentions and success criteria they can identify personal learning goals. Once the students have identified their personal learning goals, you decide to share the motivating context for the unit:

> You have your pre-assessment results back and have identified your personal learning intentions and success criteria. We are ready to start our argument-writing instruction. You are writing an argument and defending your claim in response to the prompt "Do apps help you or just waste your time?" You will be submitting your argument to the *New York Times* Learning Network editorial contest. Your argument could be published on the Internet, so your revisions are important!

In this case this is a "real and genuine" performance task, and the occupation is that of student.

As a result of your scoring of the pre-assessment, you have noted common strengths and areas that pose challenges for your students in argument writing, and you can determine the learning intentions and success criteria for the whole group, small groups, and individuals. You will basically be chunking the learning intentions and success criteria by student need. It is very possible there will be a few different priority needs, so that you might provide instruction on a common learning intention need and then, as students revise their work to meet the success criteria, you meet with small groups or individual students who have particular learning intention needs and provide mini-lessons. As students learn and revise their arguments, they will get feedback not only from you but also from their peers and from self-assessment using the scoring guide. They can determine their greatest learning needs and the success criteria on which they want to focus to improve their arguments. In this case, the learning experience is the development of the performance task. The final product can serve as a formative assessment for the next argument-writing performance task, as a summative assessment, or as both a guide for future argument-writing instruction and an evaluation of what students have learned—a grade.

It is your decision what role you want your performance task to serve. The unit standards and the knowledge, skills, and understandings you are striving to help your students grasp should be the driving forces behind how you structure your performance tasks. Even if you choose to have only a culminating performance task, this does not mean you will not be checking for knowledge, skills, and understandings periodically throughout the unit.

The simplest performance task model is to have a summative performance task at the end of the instructional unit. In this case you would determine which success criteria could be demonstrated through a performance task. It is possible that a mixture of unistructural, multistructural, relational, and extended abstract success criteria could be included—it just depends on the performance task itself. The goal is not to try to include all the success criteria but to focus on the relational and extended abstract levels, as those levels take into consideration the understandings at the surface level. If students do not have a solid understanding of the surface-level success criteria, they will be significantly challenged by the relational and extended abstract levels. Just as the development of a performance task depends on a solid base, students need a solid understanding of the surface-level learning in order to relate and extend their understanding.

For success criteria that you may not be able to include on the summative assessment, there is no harm in having a traditional assessment with multiple-choice, short-response, and extended-response questions. For assessments, the recommendation is to have 30% of the questions at the surface, 30% at the deep level, and then a mixture for the remaining 40% (Hattie, 2012). If you are creating a performance task, you should try to apply the same balance. Focus on how many surface and deep success criteria are being demonstrated through the completion of the performance task.

For the summative performance task model, you would determine which success criteria are to be included, create the performance task, and then plan your classroom instruction and formative assessments to monitor progress on the success criteria by utilizing the learning progressions. At the end of the unit, students would complete the performance task to demonstrate their level of understanding on certain success criteria. For those success criteria not included in the performance task, you could evaluate students during

Figure 5.3 Visual Representation of Summative Performance Task

Pre-Assessment—Instruction—Formative Check—Instruction—Formative Check—
Summative Performance Task

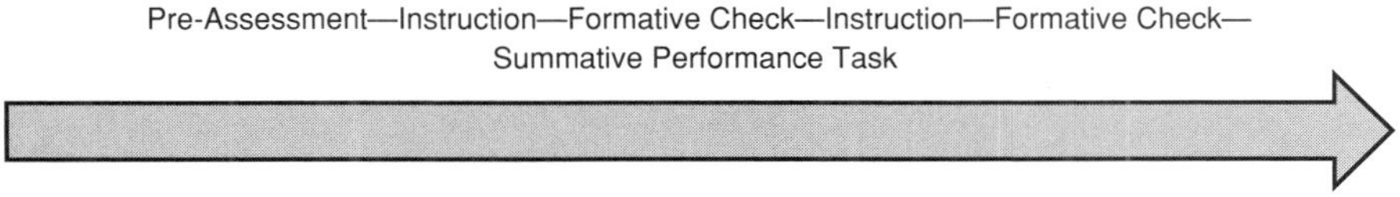

instruction or administer a traditional summative assessment in conjunction with the completion of the performance task.

The final model to consider, a combination model, can be credited to the thinking of Douglas Reeves, founder of the Center for Performance Assessment, now known as the Leadership and Learning Center. His flagship book *Making Standards Work: How to Implement Standards-Based Assessments in the Classroom, School, and District* (first published in 1997; third edition 2004) was brought to life in the form of a seminar on creating performance-based assessment held by the Leadership and Learning Center. In 2011, I had the privilege to publish *Engaging Students Through Performance Assessment: Creating Performance Tasks to Monitor Student Learning*, which was a companion book for the seminar on the same topic (Flach, 2011). This particular model consists of a series of performance tasks that increase in rigor, beginning with a focus on the surface levels of learning and progressing up to the relational level, with the final performance task focusing on the extended abstract level. Between the performance tasks, the teacher provides instruction, adjusting that instruction based on student evidence from the preceding performance task. At the same time, students are adjusting their learning strategies. The series of performance tasks offers a means of developing students' learning and application of the knowledge, concepts, and skills, leading to the completion of a culminating performance task. This process corresponds well to the hierarchical success criteria.

Think of this model as a continuum of learning. To begin, you need to determine which success criteria could be demonstrated in a real-world performance task focusing on the relational and extended abstract levels. You then must decide how many tasks are needed to scaffold the learning and what those tasks will be. You will want to refer to both your success criteria and your learning progressions to determine where you placed those formative checks for understanding. Those may serve as points for performance tasks. As for the number of tasks, it will depend on the success criteria and how those might be grouped into tasks, but a range of three to five tasks is recommended (Flach, 2011, p. 83). In this scenario, the performance tasks during instruction are formative and may be basic tasks versus

Figure 5.4 Combination of Formative Performance Tasks and a
Summative Performance Task

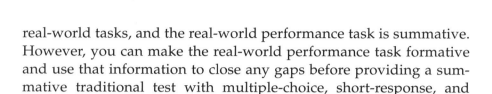

Pre-Assessment—Instruction—Task 1 (Formative), Instruction—Task 2 (Formative),
Instruction—Task 3 (Formative), Instruction—Performance Task (Summative)

real-world tasks, and the real-world performance task is summative.
However, you can make the real-world performance task formative
and use that information to close any gaps before providing a summative traditional test with multiple-choice, short-response, and
extended-response questions utilizing the SOLO success criteria.

Step 4: Developing and Designing Performance Tasks

Performance tasks can fall along a continuum from tasks such as
extended responses to authentic learning experiences that address
real-world problems and issues. Tasks are located on the continuum
based on their level of authenticity, with real-world performance
tasks being the most viable type—such performance tasks have
enough authenticity to demonstrate relevance in learning, resulting
in greater student engagement and motivation.

Several attributes need to be taken into consideration in the
development of a performance task; you may want to create a cheat
sheet or checklist to remind you of these. The performance task is
the vehicle for students to demonstrate their deep levels of
understanding—it is not about the task itself, no matter how engaging and motivating it might be. Performance tasks are optimal for
demonstrating the relational and extended abstract levels of understanding, and creating a powerful performance task is a matter of
finding the right real-world context.

1. Begin by referencing the unit standards in conjunction with
   the success criteria to determine if a product or performance
   or a combination of both is the best option. You will need to
   focus on the standards because the standards themselves can
   be directive as to what the product will be, especially with
   writing and speaking standards or visual art standards in
   which students need to "create." At the same time, you will be
   deciding on the model you will be following. For instance,
   will the product or performance be part of a learning

experience, part of a series of formative mini–performance tasks followed by a culminating real-world performance task, or solely a summative real-world performance task?

2. Once you have determined the product or performance and the model that will be used, you must decide what the specific product (e.g., research findings from a science experiment in the form of graphs and written findings) or performance (e.g., YouTube video, watercolor painting, formal oral presentation) will be. If you are using the model in which formative mini–performance tasks lead to a culminating summative performance task, you will also have to determine what the mini–performance tasks are going to be. This might be the case if you have a comprehensive project that students are completing, and you can chunk the learning and application into sections.

3. Next, you must determine what success criteria focusing on the relational and extended abstract levels of understanding can be included in the performance task. This does not mean that surface-level success criteria cannot be included in the performance task. Make a brief note in the SOLO template in the "context" area. Provide a general description of the context in which students will demonstrate their understanding of the SOLO learning intention. If you are using the model in which mini–performance tasks lead to a culminating performance task, then the mini–performance tasks will most likely be at the surface level and maybe at the relational level, with the culminating task focusing on the extended abstract level. Don't fret if you have success criteria that cannot "fit" into a performance task. You can assess those success criteria either through a different formative assessment means or by using a summative assessment in a traditional format.

4. Since you now know what the product or performance will be, the model you will use, and the success criteria that will be incorporated, it is time to write the motivating context. Be sure to include the position students are assuming (even if they are completing the task from a student perspective), the specific product or performance they will create, and the audience that will be the recipient of the product or performance.

5. Write detailed directions for students, specifying precisely how they are to complete the performance task. The detail in these directions will help you to devise the scoring guides.

6. Create any supporting materials that students will need to complete the performance task.

Sample Motivating Context and Student Directions

The elementary sample presented in Figures 5.5 and 5.6 indicates what SOLO success criteria are included in this particular performance task. The figures highlight the success criteria that students will demonstrate in their performance task. Be aware that there is a second performance task in which a number of the success criteria will be demonstrated, but it is not included in the example. Students will also be keeping a journal and be asked to respond to different writing prompts throughout the reading of the book.

Figure 5.5   SOLO Taxonomy for Grade 3, RL.3.2

SOLO Level	Unistructural: One Idea	Multistructural: Many Ideas; No Connections Between Facts and Ideas	Relational: Connections Between Facts and Ideas	Extended Abstract: Generalize Learning and Apply to Different Contexts
Student-friendly learning intention: "We are learning to . . ."	Describe characters in a story and explain how what they do affects the story line.			
SOLO Verbs	Define	Describe	Explain	Predict
Success criteria: "We are successful when we are able to . . ."	Define what a character trait is. Define what character motivation is.	Describe three characters.	Explain a character's actions and how his/her actions lead to the order of events.	Predict how the story would have changed if a character failed to take a critical action in the story.
Context for learning: "Students will engage in their learning by . . ."	Students will engage in learning by reading *Charlotte's Web* through a "book club." The book club will have guiding questions for their discussions.		Explain Charlotte's actions and how her actions lead to the order of events.	Recognizing Wilbur's character, predict what would have happened if he had been unable to convince Templeton to retrieve Charlotte's egg sac before leaving the fair.

The book club is not the main performance task, but it is a real-world task, and students will be learning through discussions around the guiding questions. I could create a motivating context around the book club as well.

Figure 5.6   SOLO Taxonomy for Grade 3, W.3.1

SOLO Level	Unistructural: One Idea	Multistructural: Many Ideas; No Connections Between Facts and Ideas	Relational: Connections Between Facts and Ideas	Extended Abstract: Generalize Learning and Apply to Different Contexts
Student-friendly learning intention: "We are learning to . . ."	Write an opinion piece and support your opinion with reasons.			
SOLO Verbs	Define/state	List and describe	Justify/apply	Reflect
Success criteria: "We are successful when we are able to . . ."	Define point of view.	List and describe three types of organizational structures.	Justify your opinion.	Reflect on your opinion.
	Define opinion.	List common linking words and phrases used when writing.	Apply an organizational structure and linking words.	
	State an opinion on a topic.			
Context for learning: "Students will engage in their learning by . . ."	Write an opinion piece on your favorite *Charlotte's Web* character.			Reflect on your opinion of Templeton. Would it change if Templeton had not retrieved Charlotte's egg sac for Wilbur? Why or why not?

Performance Task Basics

Real-World Performance Task: Written opinion

Role/Position: Student

Audience: School librarian and community members via web page

Motivating Context: Your school is celebrating the 65th anniversary of the first publication of *Charlotte's Web*. As part of the celebration, students have the opportunity to have their written opinions of their favorite characters appear on the school's web page. Get your pens ready and get reading!

Student Performance Task Directions: Mrs. Richards, the school librarian, is celebrating the 65th anniversary of the first publication of *Charlotte's Web*, by E. B. White, by asking students to write opinion pieces on their favorite *Charlotte's Web* characters, including why those characters are their favorites. From all the written submissions, Mrs. Richards will determine the favorite character among the students, and five opinion pieces will be randomly selected each week of the month to be included on the school's web page for community members to read, along with a graph of the results of the choice of the favorite character at Oakridge Elementary. The guidelines for submitting an opinion piece are as follows:

- Introduce *Charlotte's Web*.

- State an opinion on your favorite character.

- Include a description of your favorite character and his or her role in the story's events.

- Use an organizational structure to explain your opinion.

- Justify your opinion with reasons.

- Use common linking words and phrases.

- Provide a concluding statement or section.

Follow Along: Creating a Performance Task

1. It is time to revisit your template. Reference the primary standards in Step 1 to determine what product or performance would be the best option for either learning or demonstrating the learning of these unit standards.

2. At the same time, decide which model you will follow. That is, will the performance task be a learning experience, a series of formative mini–performance tasks followed by a real-world summative culminating performance task, or solely a summative real-world performance task?

3. Establish clearly what the performance task will be, such as determining how many moving boxes (of different sizes) will fit on a

tractor trailer or researching and orally presenting information. If you have formative mini–performance tasks, determine what each of those will be as well. For instance, if an oral presentation will require a lot of research, one possible mini–performance task might be an outline of the oral presentation incorporating the research. (Political speechwriters probably start with an outline before they draft speeches for their candidates.)

4. Go through each of your success criteria at each of the levels of understanding to determine which success criteria could be incorporated into the performance task. Focus on the relational and extended abstract levels, but remember that it is okay to include the surface levels of understanding as well. Do not worry if you have success criteria that are not included, as they can be assessed through other formative or summative means.

5. Now it is time to elaborate on the performance task and create the motivating context. Start by identifying the basic information as in this example:

    a. Real-world performance task: Research and write an information report that will be turned into a speech and oral presentation

    b. Position or role of student: Speechwriter for a U.S. senator (identify a senator from your state)

    c. Audience: Americans Against Fracking organization

Next is the motivating context. This example task actually has two motivating contexts, as students will be partnered up. Each student will do his or her own research.

    d. *Motivating Context 1:* Senator [Name] of [your state] is up for reelection this year and is giving a speech to the Americans Against Fracking organization. He/she is hoping for an endorsement from the organization at the end of the speech, and thus it needs to be a powerful speech. The organization would like the senator to speak on his/her position on fracking. You are the senator's speechwriter and will need to research fracking so the senator's position can be reinforced.

    e. *Motivating Context 2:* You are Senator [Name] of [your state], and you are up for reelection this year. You are scheduled to give a speech to the Americans Against Fracking organization, and you are hoping the organization will endorse you in the upcoming election. Your speechwriter is preparing a speech for you to present at a meeting of the organization.

Key Takeaways

- Several key attributes should be embedded in each and every performance task:
  - Alignment with the SOLO learning intentions and success criteria.
  - Application of knowledge, skills, and understandings (with emphasis on deep levels of learning).
  - Authenticity: The more authentic the better, but real-world performance tasks are readily available and powerful.
    - Level of authenticity is related to student relevance.
    - Relevance is related to motivation and engagement.
    - The motivating context brings authenticity, relevance, motivation, and engagement to life.
  - Integration with at least one other subject area and incorporation of 21st century skills.
  - Appropriate level of challenge.
  - Utilization of scoring guides.
- There are three model options for performance tasks:
  - A performance task may be used solely as a summative assessment.
  - A series of scaffolded formative performance tasks may be used, followed by a culminating task (formative or summative).
  - A performance task may be used as a learning experience.
- Performance tasks can result in products (written or visual works, physical models) or performances (oral, musical, dramatic, sports).

Reflection Questions

1. Which attribute do you believe has the greatest importance in the development of a performance task? Why is it more important than any of the other attributes?

2. How important is relevance of learning for the age group you teach? If you are an administrator, is relevance more important at one level than at another? Why or why not?

3. How do you envision performance tasks being utilized in your classroom?

4. What resonated with you the most in this chapter and why?

6

Scoring Guides, aka Rubrics

Scoring guides, also known as rubrics, have become commonplace in educational settings, from the classroom level to the national high-stakes assessments. It should be noted up front that not all scoring guides are truly rubrics, even though the terms are widely used interchangeably. A scoring guide is a rubric only when it includes three or more levels of quality. It is very possible that you are already familiar with a lot of the information in this chapter, but it is my hope that you will take this opportunity to review and refresh your knowledge of scoring guides/rubrics—perhaps you will glean some new insights into their creation and use in the classroom. Scoring guides are a distinguishing attribute of performance tasks, no matter whether the tasks are part of instructional learning experiences or summative assessments.

Scoring Guide Synopsis

Scoring guides are the means through which performance task products and performances are evaluated. They are closely connected to the success criteria, as well as to the directions created for students to guide them in completing performance tasks. Giselle Martin-Kniep (2000) defines a rubric as a product that "identifies all the needed attributes of quality or development in a process, product or performance, and defines different levels for each of these attributes" (p. 34). The attributes of quality and the different levels of quality can be organized in two different ways: holistically or analytically. The "attributes" are called descriptors, or criteria, for the product or performance, and typically three to six levels of quality are described, depending on the age level of the student. Both holistic and analytical scoring guides have levels of quality for the product, performance, or process and criteria that describe each of the levels of quality. Either holistic or analytical scoring guides can be used with performance tasks—the type you should use will depend on whether your performance task is formative or summative (Brookhart, 2015).

If you are familiar with W. James Popham's writing, you will not be surprised by his definition of a rubric, as he is a straight shooter. Popham (2003) states, "A rubric is a scoring guide that's intended to help those who must score students' responses to constructed-response items" (p. 95). Even though scoring guides have become more prevalent in education for constructed-response items (short responses, extended responses, performances, and products), they may not always be well written and thus not always as effective as they potentially could be. You need to be aware of the qualities that can make scoring guides soar high in the sky versus crash and burn. If you are able to create a high-quality scoring guide, as well as discern a good scoring guide from a bad one, you and your students will reap the benefits. This is not to say that everything about scoring guides is beneficial—the use of scoring guides can have some detriments as well. You will need to decide whether the benefits outweigh the detriments.

Holistic Scoring Guides

As the word *holistic* implies, with a holistic scoring guide the performance task is evaluated as a whole, and the score is indicative of the level of quality (such as a score of 3 on a scoring guide with four levels). Evaluating the performance task as a whole typically means that series of criteria represent each of the designated levels. Holistic scoring guides are used to evaluate performance tasks, or other types of constructed responses, extended or short, in their entirety rather than by designated components such as organization and content. Because the scorer has only one set of criteria to look at on each of the levels, holistic scoring guides are not as time-consuming to create or as challenging for scorers to use as are analytical scoring guides (Ainsworth, 2015; Brookhart, 2015; Burke, 2011; Martin-Kniep, 2000; Wiggins & McTighe, 2005).

Holistic scoring guides also save time because they keep all the focus on the performance level that represents meeting the success criteria, or what has typically been known as "proficiency." Figure 6.1

displays a four-level holistic scoring guide utilizing a format that keeps the focus on the "proficient" or Meets Success Criteria level of quality.

The process of writing a holistic scoring guide starts with the writing of the criteria that describe the level of performance deemed to meet the success criteria—and that is what the level is labeled: "Meets Success Criteria." The next level to complete is "Exceeds Success Criteria." This includes additional criteria that make the product or performance superior, going beyond simply meeting the success criteria. In order for students to achieve this higher level, they must meet all of the criteria at the Meets Success Criteria level plus the additional criteria listed in the Exceeds Success Criteria level. (As Figure 6.1 shows, it is not necessary to write a full set of

Figure 6.1   Holistic Telling Time Scoring Guide

You can decide what to name the levels and how many levels to incorporate into your scoring guide. The levels can be names, numbers, or even symbols, depending on the grade level.

The descriptors describe each of the levels of quality. How to write descriptors will be discussed in an upcoming section. Be careful of the number of criteria descriptors—if you have more than 6 or 7 descriptors you may want to consider an analytical scoring guide.

Exceeds Success Criteria	*Meets Success Criteria*	*Approaching Meets Success Criteria*	*A Long Way From Meets Success Criteria*
Everything in Meets Success Criteria, Plus: • Writes the correct time from analog and digital clocks to the exact minute. • Verbally states the correct time from analog and digital clocks to the exact minute.	• Writes the correct time to the nearest five minutes from a digital clock. • Writes the correct time to the nearest five minutes from an analog clock. • Verbally states the correct time to the nearest five minutes from a digital clock. • Verbally states the correct time to the nearest five minutes from an analog clock. • Includes a.m. and p.m. in written and oral format.	• At least 3 Meets Success Criteria have been attained.	• Fewer than 3 Meets Success Criteria have been attained.

When using this format, it is not necessary to write criteria for levels below Meets Success Criteria, because this level refers back to Meets Success Criteria.

criteria at each level.) The next level that is completed is one level below Meets Success Criteria, labeled "Approaching Meets Success Criteria." The criteria for this level are based on those at the Meets Success Criteria level. For instance, if five criteria are listed for Meets Success Criteria (as in Figure 6.1) and a student is approaching this level, that student should be meeting three or four of the success criteria. In a four-level scoring guide the remaining level, the lowest, is also based on the Meets Success Criteria level. This lowest level is labeled "A Long Way From Meets Success Criteria"; a student who meets fewer than three of the criteria under Meets Success Criteria would be at this level.

An added benefit of developing scoring guides in this manner is that it helps you to keep the language objective. When you are writing criteria for every level of a scoring guide, it is challenging not to use subjective language (such as *minimally, limited, sometimes, occasionally*) in distinguishing between levels. The importance of using objective language in scoring guides is discussed further below.

Analytical Scoring Guides

Analytical scoring guides provide an additional level of specificity, as they "disaggregate the parts of a product or performance into its critical attributes or dimensions" (Martin-Kniep, 2000, p. 35). Each of the dimensions identified in the scoring guide has descriptors at each of the levels. Figure 6.2 provides an example of the layout of an analytical scoring guide. The most well-known analytical scoring guide is the 6+1 Trait Writing scoring guide developed by the Northwest Regional Education Laboratory, now known as Education Northwest. In 2014, Education Northwest released revised 6+1 Trait scoring guides to align with the Common Core State Standards. Analytical scoring guides are best used when the performance tasks, or other types of responses, are formative and specific feedback is desirable.

To develop an analytical scoring guide, you can proceed in the same manner as that described above for a holistic scoring guide, focusing on the level "Meets Success Criteria." In this case, each dimension will have its own Meets Success Criteria. There may not be many criteria for each dimension—that will depend on what the task entails and what the success criteria state. This can be problematic when you are defining the lower levels of the scoring guide. Compared with holistic scoring guides, analytical rubrics have a greater level of specificity in regard to quality, and they can provide feedback so students and teachers can make adjustments, but they tend to be more challenging to develop, because of the specificity needed, and longer to score, since essentially you are providing a score for each dimension.

Figure 6.2   Analytical Oral Presentation Scoring Guide

There are two dimensions to this scoring guide, but there could be more. It is a matter of the level of specificity needed.

An analytical scoring guide adds specificity through the dimensions. If this were holistic, there would be eight criteria listed with no delineation between content and delivery.

Dimension	Exceeds Success Criteria	Meets Success Criteria	Approaching Meets Success Criteria	A Long Way From Meets Success Criteria
Content	Everything in Meets Success Criteria, Plus: • Content is enhanced through multimedia. • More than three supporting points explained.	• Content is organized. • Content is focused on a topic or purpose. • Content is accurate. • At least three supporting points explained.	At least 3 Meets Success Criteria have been attained.	Fewer than 3 Meets Success Criteria have been attained.
Delivery	Everything in Meets Success Criteria, Plus: • Posture exudes confidence. • Glances at notes.	• Voice level projects. • Eye contact connects with the entire audience. • Gestures support but do not distract from presentation. • Pronunciation is clear.	At least 3 Meets Success Criteria have been attained.	Fewer than 3 Meets Success Criteria have been attained.

Scoring Guides for the Next Generation Assessments

Since the Next Generation Assessments of PARCC and SBAC have performance tasks in both English language arts and mathematics, scoring guides are provided to accompany them. The English language arts scoring guides both happen to be analytical rather than holistic, including two to three dimensions, with each dimension having criteria. The mathematics scoring guides for both SBAC and PARCC are typically based on a point system ranging from zero to 2 or 3 points and are specific to each math problem or component of an extended problem. These would not be considered rubrics because they do not have the required levels of quality.

The SBAC performance tasks in English language arts focus on writing in one of three areas, depending on grade level: narrative, informative/explanatory, or opinion/argumentative. PARCC's performance-based assessment (PBA) is administered in the spring, prior to the end-of-year summative assessment. The PBA is broken down into three writing tasks: a "Research Simulation Task," a "Literary Analysis Task," and a "Narrative Writing Task." The SBAC performance task writing rubrics for grades 3–11 are analytical, with three dimensions and four levels. The three areas of writing, mentioned above, all have the same three dimensions: "Purpose/Organization," "Evidence/Elaboration," and "Conventions." Depending on the area of writing (narrative, informative/explanatory, or opinion/argumentative), there are different descriptors, or criteria, for grades 3–5, 3–8, and 6–11. The SBAC assessments include holistic scoring guides for conventions that range from a score of zero to a score of 2; scoring is based on the variety of errors, the severity of errors, and the density of errors. There is also a "no score" option. The PARCC assessments include only two dimensions in their analytical scoring guides, which span grades 3 through 11: "Reading Comprehension/Written Expression" and "Knowledge of Language and Conventions." The descriptors vary depending on the grade-level span, which is broken into grade 3 on its own, grades 4–5, and grades 6–11. (For more on the Next Generation Assessments, see the PARCC and SBAC websites: http://www.parcconline.org and http://www.smarterbalanced.org.)

Benefits of Scoring Guides

Each type of scoring guide, holistic and analytical, has specific benefits, as noted above, but the benefits of scoring guides in general do not end there. Both students and teachers alike will profit from the use of well-constructed scoring guides. Among the greatest benefits of scoring guides are that they generate effective feedback, enhance grading fairness, and contribute to the development of assessment-capable learners.

Effective Feedback

As a result of developing a proper base for your performance task, you have generated clear learning intentions and success criteria—the basis for the development of the scoring guides. When done well, feedback is a powerful influence on student achievement, with an effect size of 0.75 (Hattie, 2012). Reflecting on my own K–12 education, as well as my college undergraduate years, I realize that at no point in time did a teacher share a scoring guide with a class, or even use a scoring guide to evaluate a written product, such as an essay or written response to a word problem. Often there would be a capital B written in red pen at the top of an essay, along with generic comments such as "Nice work." The closest thing to any useful feedback of any kind that I can remember getting was along the lines of "Be careful of your grammar usage." "Grammar usage" is rather broad, don't you think? Did I need to work on commas, apostrophes, or something else? With such comments I did not know what I did well, or what grammar issues I needed to focus on to improve my next essay. I was just cognizant of the fact that what I wrote had grammar issues. A scoring guide, especially an analytical one, would have provided me with more specific feedback on what I needed to improve and learn next.

Feed Up, Feed Back, and Feed Forward

John Hattie and Helen Timperley provide a useful discussion of feedback in their article "The Power of Feedback" (2007). As these authors note, the purpose of feedback is "to reduce discrepancies between current understandings and performance and a goal" (p. 86). Closing the gap comes down to how effective students and teachers are at reducing the discrepancies between current understandings and the goal. Effective feedback answers the three critical questions for students and teachers: "Where am I going?" (feed up), "How am I going?" (feedback), and "Where to next?" (feed forward).

Both teachers and students need to be cognizant of what the goals are, and as a result of the development of clear learning intentions and success criteria, students and teachers can respond with confidence to the prompt "Where am I going?" (Hattie & Timperley, 2007). Remember, teacher clarity has a student achievement effect size of 0.75. It is amazing that the simple activity of sharing with students what they will be learning and what defines success in attaining the learning can have such a powerful impact (Hattie, 2012). The learning intentions and success criteria represent a road map for student learning—a means of "feeding up."

When students and teachers utilize the success criteria and scoring guides for performance tasks to evaluate progress, they reveal successes as well as discrepancies, or gaps, in knowledge and application (Hattie & Timperley, 2007). Both teachers and students can be responsible for reducing the discrepancies once progress in meeting the learning goals has been monitored. When students monitor their progress against the success criteria and scoring guides they can answer the question "How am I going?" and can obtain feedback from the teacher, peers, or themselves. As noted previously, the use of learning logs can support the development of assessment-capable learners. By using learning logs, students can monitor their progress and reflect on strategies and learning. Yes, I admit it, this is a plug for learning logs. In my former position as a middle school remedial reading teacher, I utilized a reading menu and written reflections, a version of learning logs. Students would select their pre-reading strategies based on their purposes of reading, then select during-reading strategies that allowed for monitoring of comprehension, and finally select post-reading strategies to further process their reading. The intent was to develop metacognitive readers, and learning logs are a means of developing metacognitive learners who are in control of their learning—active rather than passive learners.

Once students and teachers have monitored progress, they can answer the question "Where to next?" (feed forward; Hattie & Timperley, 2007). Students can adjust their learning strategies or revise their goals, and teachers can ensure the goals are appropriately challenging as well as "feed forward" by suggesting learning strategies that will support student progress to the next level of learning.

Feedback Levels

Hattie and Timperley (2007) outline four levels of feedback, which vary in their effectiveness: task level, process level, self-regulation level, and self level. All of these kinds of feedback have distinctive characteristics and target different aspects of learning. The four levels are also integral to Hattie's discussion of feedback in *Visible Learning for Teachers* (2012).

After you have read the information below on the levels of feedback, you might want to ask a colleague or an administrator to visit your classroom to observe and report to you on the level of feedback you are verbally providing to students. Or you might want to record yourself on video as you teach some classes, so you can self-assess your use of feedback. If you decide to record yourself, be sure to inform your students that the video is only of you and is for your learning. You can do a similar kind of self-assessment by reviewing written work that has been submitted as well. You have to know where you are now in order to determine where you need to make adjustments in your feedback to students. If you are not familiar with the four levels of feedback, it might be a challenge to adjust your behaviors, but if you have gathered some pre-assessment data on your current level of feedback, you will know how big the discrepancy is between your current application and the desirable application of the three most powerful levels of feedback—task, process, and self-regulation.

Feedback at the task level is concerned with the task or product being completed and whether or not it has been done correctly. Such feedback often targets better understanding of the surface-level knowledge. Task feedback is often referred to as corrective feedback. It is probably the most common kind of feedback that occurs in classrooms. This type of feedback can be very clear to students as they are working on completing their performance task product or performance, especially when students have misunderstood the performance task directions; after receiving task-level feedback, they have the opportunity to make corrections and revisions. Task feedback can serve as a building block for feedback at the process and self-regulation levels. A limitation of task-level feedback is that it is specific to a given task and does not typically transfer from task to task.

Recall the example from Chapter 5 of the seventh-grade performance task of writing an argument to the prompt, "Do apps help you or just waste your time?" to be submitted to the *New York Times* Learning Network blog's contest. One of the success criteria for this performance task is to state a claim. Marcus states in his introduction that some apps are helpful and other apps are a waste of time, and he goes on to support both sides. Task feedback to Marcus might sound like this: "Marcus, take a look at your claim. Does it meet the success criterion? Is it clear which statement you believe and support over the other? Is it that apps are helpful or that they waste people's time?" Either Marcus has not clearly understood the task or he is not clear on how to state a claim on a topic when writing an argument.

The teacher in this example could provide this task feedback during revision time on an individual basis, unless multiple students have shown the same lack of understanding, in which case the feedback could be provided in a small group.

The next type of feedback, at the process level, focuses on how to complete the task, whether it is a product or a performance. With process-level feedback, students are applying the surface-level knowledge, skills, and concepts, and they may need this type of feedback so they can make connections between ideas or use particular strategies across different situations. Providing process feedback helps students move into the deeper levels of understanding as they are learning to apply the surface knowledge, skills, and concepts. Process feedback targets how students approach the application.

This is what feedback at the process level might sound like to a seventh-grade student who has used Wikipedia as her main source of evidence to support her argument: "Cecily, what sources did you use to support your claim? Did you consider them to be credible sources, and why? Did more than one source come to the same conclusion?" Process feedback can help students make connections between the surface-level knowledge, skills, and concepts; guide students to discern errors or to learn from their errors; and encourage students to try different strategies. This particular process feedback is intended to help Cecily realize that to support a claim she should cite multiple credible sources of information and not rely on just one source.

Feedback at the self-regulation level targets students' ability to monitor their learning processes and their effectiveness. When you are self-monitoring, you are assessing your own progress in meeting the success criteria and making adjustments based on that self-assessment. The success criteria and the scoring guide are the tools that students use in order to self-monitor, determine what they need to do next in order to progress, and adjust their learning processes or strategies. It is interesting that self-monitoring and self-assessment are means for students to formatively assess themselves, but the only way students can do this is with teacher clarity of the learning intentions and success criteria as well as scoring guides for the performances or products being developed. If students are not aware of where they are going (learning intentions) or how they will

> Feedback at this level can enhance students' skills in self-evaluation, provide greater confidence to engage further with the task, assist in the student seeking and accepting feedback, and enhance the willingness to invest effort into seeking and dealing with feedback information. (Hattie, 2012, p. 120)

know when they have gotten there (success criteria), they cannot self-regulate their learning. Self-regulation feedback helps to develop assessment-capable learners and builds on student self-efficacy, which is a student's belief that he or she can attain the learning goal.

Self-regulation feedback to a seventh grader who has responded to an argument prompt and has reached the Meets Success Criteria level on the scoring guide may sound like this: "Jennifer, what do you think you will do differently the next time you're asked to write an argument?" This question encourages Jennifer to reflect on her learning and self-assess her strengths and determine areas for improvement the next time she writes an argument. Jennifer is being encouraged to self-regulate her learning.

The final type of feedback, at the self level, focuses on the person versus the learning and often comes in the form of praise. This is the least effective form of feedback in Hattie and Timperley's (2007) model; however, it was the most common type of feedback I received as a student back in the 1970s and 1980s. Yes, that was a number of years ago, and a lot of things have changed, but I believe such feedback is still all too common. At the beginning of this section on feedback I challenged you to gather some baseline evidence on the level of feedback you are providing students. Take me up on that challenge. In the meantime, if you have smiley face stickers or stamps in your classroom, or stamps that say "Good job!" ditch them, or at least limit the use of them. Even if you also provide task, process, or self-regulation feedback, as soon as that smiley face hits the page, the student will focus on that and not on the other feedback (Hattie, 2012). If you have a tendency to write generic phrases on student papers such as "Great work," "Nice job," or "Try harder next time," *stop!* When you do that, you are focusing on the student as a person versus the learning and progress of the student. As Hattie (2012) states: "The message is that for feedback to be effective in the act of learning, praise dissipates the message. Praise the students to make them feel welcomed to your class and worthwhile as learners, but if you wish to make a difference to learning, leave praise out of feedback about learning" (p. 121). The bottom line is, keep praise separate from the three effective types of feedback: task, process, and self-regulation. If Ms. Richland wants to praise one of her students, Raphael, for pitching a great baseball game yesterday, she should not do so when she sits down with him to conference on his writing prompt, at which point she needs to provide task feedback. Such praise is better shared with Raphael and the class as Ms. Richland greets them at the door as they enter the classroom.

Providing effective feedback is challenging, but it is a beneficial practice that should be present in every classroom. Gather some baseline data so you can measure your learning progress. Walk the talk and show your students you are a lifelong learner of teaching, always trying to improve your craft so you can provide them with the best educational experience.

Grading Fairness

Even though I enjoyed completing performance tasks that would have fallen at various points along the performance task continuum during my K–12 school years—including writing a research paper on mountain lions, building a wine rack for my parents, and writing a poem in Old English after reading *Beowulf*—in most cases a numeric or letter grade was provided, and I had no idea why I received the grade I did, because grades on products and performances were completely subjective. Was my poem the first one of several Dr. Fountain had read that actually resembled an Old English *Beowulf*-style poem? Was Mr. Schwartz being nitpicky about grammar and punctuation when he gave me a C on my mountain lion research project? Who knows? The success criteria for all of these products were in the individual minds of the teachers, and I was no mind reader. Fortunately, scoring guides have come to the rescue, but they are helpful only if they are well written.

The use of scoring guides can enhance teachers' fairness in grading products and performances because the criteria descriptors in scoring guides can eliminate a lot of subjectivity. Last summer, we had dinner at a fabulous restaurant in Charleston, South Carolina. I had gag grouper with fennel and blood orange, and it was delicious; the presentation was gorgeous as well. However, that is my personal subjective opinion. If the dish had incorporated any type of bell pepper, my opinion would have changed radically, because I have a strong dislike for peppers. On the Food Network show *Chopped,* the celebrity chef judges have at least three dimensions on which to assess the dishes created by the contestants: presentation, taste, and transformation of the mystery ingredient. However, there are no criteria specified within each of those dimensions, so the judges' personal opinions can cloud their judgment. One judge, Scott Conant, has repeatedly expressed his disdain for raw red onions. What kind of appraisal is a contestant's dish likely to get from Conant if raw red onion shows up on his plate? Luckily, there are three judges, so Conant's opinion may be balanced by those of the other two.

Figure 6.3 Subjective Language to Avoid in Scoring Guides

- Some
- Few
- Many
- Limited
- Well supported
- Adequate
- Vague
- Consistent

- Numerous
- Clearly
- Partial
- Effective
- Appropriate
- A lot
- Poorly
- Minimal

If all teachers on the same grade- or course-level team are using the same well-written, collaboratively developed scoring guide, there will be consistency in the grading process, resulting in fair and equitable grading of students. The key is to use descriptors (criteria) that are as objective as possible, no matter whether the scoring guide is holistic or analytical. Unfortunately, many of the scoring guides available online and in teacher resources are riddled with subjective language as shown in Figure 6.3. Do a search for yourself, and see if you can pick out the subjective words. Such poorly written scoring guides result in inconsistent and subjective grading of products and performances, since the subjective language is open to each person's own interpretation. If you are using rubrics from text series or online sources, be sure to take a critical eye to them to determine how objective they are.

Additionally, student self- and peer evaluations should not be done with subjectively worded scoring guides, as different interpretations of the language are possible. As a result, students will not have a true picture of how they are progressing in attaining the success criteria. Consistency in scoring products and performances is further enhanced when teachers collaboratively score student work to ensure a common understanding of each of the criteria (Burke, 2011). Well-written scoring guides that use objective language support fairness and equity in the evaluation of students' learning and progress.

Development of Assessment-Capable Learners

The importance of developing assessment-capable learners cannot be stressed enough—as noted previously, the development of such learners has an effect size of 1.44, which is off the charts! Assessment-capable learners are in control of their learning. They know what they are learning, self-assess their learning to know how they are progressing, and make decisions on where they are going next in their learning. When students are assessment capable, learning is not something that is just done to them; rather, they are actively engaged in the learning process with their teachers. Students need to take an active part in the learning process and not be passive receptacles. Shirley Clarke (2001, 2008), John Hattie (2012), Russell J. Quaglia and Michael J. Corso (2014), and Michael Fullan and Maria Langworthy (2014) are just a few of the highly distinguished educational thought leaders who have written about the power of active student engagement in the learning process and the importance of students having a voice that is heard.

Scoring guides support the development of assessment-capable learners by helping students answer the questions "How am I going?" and "Where to next?" Scoring guides enable teachers and students to evaluate student products and performances objectively against specified criteria. The completion of a product or performance is a means of demonstrating the level of student understanding of the success criteria, and the scoring guide criteria are based on the success criteria. Scoring guides encourage students to self-monitor their progress in completing products or performances to the level of quality they are aiming to meet. When teachers communicate the learning intentions and success criteria to students at the start of the unit and during individual lessons, the students know what they are learning and can determine what learning tactics they need to employ to meet the success criteria for the learning intentions.

The use of scoring guides in evaluating performance tasks completed by students can have powerful benefits for students and teachers, but scoring guides have to be well written to reap the greatest benefits. The considerations that go into the creation of a useful scoring guide are the topic of the following section.

Scoring Guide Considerations

Holistic Versus Analytical

The first determination you will need to make when writing a scoring guide for your performance task is whether the scoring guide will be holistic or analytical. As mentioned earlier, a holistic scoring guide looks at the performance or product in its entirety; thus, it has only levels of performance and descriptors, or criteria, written under each of the identified levels of performance. Such a scoring guide is best used for summative tasks, as feedback may not be as specific.

For an analytical scoring guide, you need to determine the dimensions, in addition to the levels, of performance and then write criteria for each dimension at each level. You can decide whether you want to write criteria for all levels or base the levels lower than "Meets Success Criteria" on the level indicative of a successful product or performance. Analytical scoring guides provide greater feedback to students and teachers than do holistic scoring guides; thus, analytical scoring guides are beneficial when performance tasks are used formatively. Such guides also clearly reveal to students where they need to go next with their learning. The purpose and use of the performance task will influence the type of scoring guide that you need to develop.

Levels of Performance and Proficiency

Once you have decided whether your scoring guide is going to be holistic or analytical, you need to determine how many performance levels it should include. The most common number of levels of quality for a performance task is four. For primary students you may have three, and as you move into high school you may want to use five or six. The English language arts scoring guides for both SBAC and PARCC have four levels of performance. The challenge to adding levels of performance is that you have to delineate the objective descriptors for each of those levels. Your decision about the number of levels will depend on the performance task itself and the purpose the scoring guide will serve.

Scoring guides can be used for processes in addition to products and presentations. It would be a struggle to delineate five or six levels on a scoring guide for collaborative group work that teams could use to self-assess their skills. For such a scoring guide, four levels would be appropriate. You should not attempt to create a rubric for every classroom process. Scoring guides are best used for determining progress on performance tasks, such as a variety of writing tasks, oral presentations, and projects.

In conjunction with the number of performance levels, you will need to make a few other decisions when writing a scoring guide. First, will the levels simply be numbered 4, 3, 2, and 1, along with a "no response" (NR) option, or will the levels have descriptive labels, such as "exemplary," "high," "medium," and "low" (again, along with "no response")? Once you have determined the number of levels and their labels, it is time to decide which level is representative of meeting the success criteria. The word *proficient* has typically been used to indicate student success, but it has recently come under criticism as being subjective in nature and thus open to interpretation (Ainsworth, 2015). The goal is for the students to attain the success criteria that have been identified for the learning intentions. The level that is representative of success criteria descriptors and demonstrates attainment of the learning intentions is the level of performance at which students meet the success criteria.

Sharing Scoring Guides

Often teachers are hesitant to share scoring guides with students because they think they are "giving away answers," but the criteria are organized into levels of quality, and thus there is no correct versus incorrect response option. The SOLO taxonomy was developed to determine the level of understanding demonstrated by the responses of different students to the same prompt, which can vary greatly. Even if students have the scoring guide, this does not mean their responses will meet the criteria on the scoring guide. It all depends on their level of understanding of the knowledge, skills, and concepts and their application of those in the performance task. So don't hold back—make the scoring guide transparent to students so they know what they are aiming to achieve. Students should not be forced to play a guessing game.

Self-Assessment and Peer Assessment: Two Peas in a Pod

A scoring guide is a tool for delineating the success criteria at different levels of quality. Using the scoring guide, students are able to answer the questions "How am I going?" and "Where to next?"—that is, they can track their progress toward attaining the success criteria. This can be accomplished through self-assessment as well as peer assessment. Having another set of eyes assess a product or performance you have created provides a different perspective. Peers often see what you don't, because you have become so close to the product or performance while preparing it. For instance, it was not until after reviewers provided feedback on an early draft of this book that I realized I had a tendency to start sentences with "So, . . ." I had never noticed that as I worked on the book before I submitted it for review. Thank heavens for the revision process in writing.

The success criteria, as well as the scoring guide for the performance task, serve as the guide for students to self-monitor their progress. Self-evaluation is a metacognitive strategy, and such strategies have a student achievement effect size of 0.69, well into the zone of desired effects. As Hattie (2009) explains, "Meta-cognitive activities can include planning how to approach a given learning task, evaluating progress, and monitoring comprehension" (p. 188). Students can employ a number of different strategies in conducting self-assessment, such as using highlighters or colored pencils to mark descriptors in the scoring guide as well as the evidence of their progress (Brookhart, 2013). This particular strategy would be sufficient for a written product, but not necessarily for a visual product or a performance. Incorporating space on the scoring guide for feedback is another option you might consider. Such space allows students, teachers, and peers to make notes on what might need to be improved or what was done exceptionally well.

Peer assessment is another means through which students can give and receive feedback. A scoring guide serves a few purposes during peer assessment. First, it helps to focus the conversation on the criteria versus a student's general opinion of the product or performance. Second, it serves as a crutch for the conversation, as the peer providing feedback can rely on the language of the criteria within the scoring guide. For both students, the giving and receiving of feedback furthers their understanding of the scoring guide.

Peer assessment is an additional opportunity for students to become active learners in the classroom. However, you should be aware that peer assessment is most successful in classrooms where the culture is reflective of accepting errors, mistakes, and constructive feedback as learning opportunities rather than failures (Brookhart, 2013). If you believe your students would be accepting of peer feedback, provide some direct instruction on how peers should interact during the feedback process. Model a peer feedback interaction, with a student assuming the position of a student giving feedback and yourself as the student receiving it. The more opportunities students have with peer assessment, the more confidence they will gain as learners and as peer reviewers.

Student Co-Constructed Scoring Guides

The development of scoring guides to accompany performance tasks does not have to be done solely by the teacher; scoring guides may be co-created by the teacher and the students. For that matter, the success criteria for the learning intentions can be co-constructed as well. Assessment-capable learners are involved in their learning process, and Anne Davies (2007) promotes involving students in the development of both formative and summative assessments. Davies lists "four cornerstones" that ground her work in purposefully involving students in the classroom assessment process: "formative classroom assessment, feedback, motivation, and summative evalua-tion" (p. 31). One of the strategies she highlights is teacher–student co-construction of the criteria for scoring guides. Davies notes: "Research shows that when students are involved in the assessment process—by co-constructing the criteria by which they are assessed, self-assessing in relation to the criteria, giving themselves informa-tion to guide (or 'feed-forward') their learning, collecting and pre-senting evidence of their learning, and reflecting on their strengths and needs—they learn more, achieve at higher levels, and are more motivated" (p. 31). Sign me up for co-constructing success criteria and performance task scoring guides.

Among the benefits of students and teachers co-constructing the scoring guides for performance tasks is that this process guarantees that the language is "student-friendly," which means that students have a better understanding of the expectations. It also provides the teacher with insights into what students already know and under-stand, so to some extent it is a means of tapping into student prior knowledge. When students co-create scoring guides, they are shar-ing their ideas and finding out if they are accurate or need revision.

You can support students in the process of co-constructing criteria by showing examples (Davies, 2007). You might start with an exem-plar that meets the success criteria, and then, once the criteria have been established, show other examples and ask students to assess whether they meet the co-constructed success criteria. This kind of student involvement motivates students and keeps them engaged in the learning process and their own learning. When they understand that they have a voice in the learning process, and it is not just being done to them, students are motivated to take ownership over their learning.

Step 5: Developing Performance Task Scoring Guides

Before you can actually write the descriptors for your scoring guide, you will need to make decisions about some of the considerations discussed above. Here are a few guiding questions to get you started in the process:

1. Will the scoring guide be holistic or analytical?

2. How many levels of performance will the scoring guide have?

3. Which level meets the success criteria, or demonstrates proficiency?

4. Will you have students co-construct the scoring guide descriptors (criteria)? If so, do you have an example of a product or performance that meets the success criteria to share with students to help them co-construct the descriptors?

Once you have answered these questions, you can begin the process of writing the criteria. If you are creating an analytical scoring guide, however, you will first need to determine the dimensions.

1. Write the criteria (descriptors) for the level that meets the success criteria (proficient) first. If you are creating an analytical scoring guide, write the criteria for the Meets Success Criteria level for each of the dimensions before moving on.

2. After you have completed the Meets Success Criteria level, move to the level(s) above that, which might be called "Exceeds Success Criteria," and write those descriptors. For ease and to keep the focus on meeting the success criteria minimally, use the phrase "Everything in Meets Success Criteria, Plus" and then list the descriptors. This emphasizes that students have to meet the success criteria as well as any additional criteria you add in order to reach the Exceeds Success Criteria level. When you follow this process, you do not have to repeat descriptors (criteria) for every level. All descriptors are connected to the Meets Success Criteria level. If you are writing an analytical scoring guide, you need to follow the same process for each dimension.

3. After you have written the descriptors for the level(s) above Meets Success Criteria, your focus will shift to the levels below. Start with the first level below Meets Success Criteria and work your way down. Just as Exceeds Success Criteria focuses on the Meets Success Criteria level, so do the lower levels. Count up how many descriptors you have in Meets Success Criteria, and for the level just below, decide how many of these must be met for this level; then state, "[insert numerical range] of Meets Success Criteria have been attained." For example, if you have 10 descriptors in Meets Success Criteria, the level right below would state, "6–9 of Meets Success Criteria have been attained." On each of the

successive levels below, the range will be lower. The lowest level would state, "At least 2 of Meets Success Criteria have been attained."

The benefit of this process for writing descriptors is that all levels refer back to the Meets Success Criteria level; you do not have to write descriptors for all levels, which means that the likelihood of using subjective language is reduced.

Elementary Example Scoring Guide: Opinion Writing on *Charlotte's Web*

The particular scoring guide offered here as an example is task specific. It can easily be converted into a generic opinion scoring guide, however, as only the first two descriptors in Meets Success Criteria indicate that it is task specific. In the first criterion, "*Charlotte's Web*" could be replaced with "Topic," and in the second, the words "of favorite character" could be deleted. With those two changes, this becomes a scoring guide that can be used with opinion writing throughout the year.

Figure 6.4   Grade 3 Opinion Writing Scoring Holistic Scoring Guide

Exceeds Success Criteria	*Meets Success Criteria*	*Approaching Meets Success Criteria*	*A Long Way From Meets Success Criteria*
Everything in Meets Success Criteria, Plus: • More than 2 reasons are stated. • Simple, compound, and complex sentences are used.	• *Charlotte's Web* is introduced. • Opinion of favorite character is stated. • Organizational structure lists reasons for opinion. • Opinion is supported with at least two reasons. • Common linking words and phrases are used. • A concluding statement or section is used.	At least 4 of 6 Meets Success Criteria have been attained.	1–3 of Meets Success Criteria have been attained.

Follow Along: Creating a Performance Task Scoring Guide

The process outlined below is designed to help you develop one or more scoring guides for your performance task. You may need two scoring guides, for example, if your performance task involves writing followed by a presentation. If you have selected the combination of formative performance tasks leading to a summative performance task, you will need to develop a scoring guide for each formative performance task as well as for the summative performance task. The directions below apply to each performance task scoring guide you develop.

- Determine whether your scoring guide will be analytical or holistic. Establish the number of levels and the labels of the levels. Consider aiming for four levels whenever possible. Four levels of quality is a sufficient number, as when you add more the nuances between the levels are minuscule, and the challenge of writing objective criteria becomes much greater. If you are constructing an analytical scoring guide, you will also need to determine dimensions.
- Determine which level should be representative of meeting the success criteria. Using objective language and relying on the student performance task directions and requirements, which should be reflective of the success criteria, write the criteria for the Meets Success Criteria level (or the equivalent level, whatever you have labeled it).
  - o You can use a combination of qualitative and quantitative criteria. For example, "A claim is stated in the introduction" or "Three details support the main idea." Do not specify numbers of grammatical errors; rather, focus on the impact of the grammar on the readability and clarity of the writing. Using numbers to delineate one level of quality from another in respect to grammar becomes nitpicky.

- Your next step will depend on whether you have decided to write criteria for each level of the scoring guide or to have all levels refer back to the Meets Success Criteria level.
  - o If you are writing objective criteria for each level, proceed to the level(s) above the Meets Success Criteria level and write those criteria.
  - o If all levels refer back to the Meets Success Criteria level, proceed to the level above (Exceeds Success Criteria) and use

the phrase "Everything in Meets Success Criteria, Plus," then write the additional criteria for that level. If you have two levels above, then for the highest level use the wording "Everything in Meets Success Criteria and Exceeds Success Criteria, Plus" and write the additional criteria for that level.

- Next, proceed to the first level below Meets Success Criteria. Continue with the same version of criteria writing you have selected.
    - If you are writing all the criteria for each level, start with the level below Meets Success Criteria and write the criteria for this level. Proceed to any other levels that are below and write the criteria.
    - If all levels refer back to Meets Success Criteria, in the first level below use the phrase "[numerical range] of Meets Success Criteria have been attained." Count how many criteria you have in Meets Success Criteria, and based on that number determine minimally how many are needed for the "approaching" level. For instance, if you have 10 criteria in Meets Success Criteria, you might decide that a student needs to attain at least 8 to be considered to be approaching meeting the success criteria. If you have 4 criteria, then attaining 3 would probably reach the "approaching" level. There is no distinction that one criterion is more important than any another, as these are based on the success criteria. Continue the process with the levels below. If there are two or more levels below, the lowest level would use the phrase "Fewer than [the number used to minimally meet the level above] Meets Success Criteria have been attained." For example, if the level above is "3 out of 8 Meets Success Criteria have been attained," the lowest level would be "Fewer than 3 Meets Success Criteria have been attained." If you do not want to include a zero in the lowest level, you may want to consider a "no response" (NR) level and rephrase your lowest level to "Between 1 and 2 Meets Success Criteria have been attained."

In developing performance task scoring guides, you may want to use the examples in Figures 6.1 and 6.2 as guidance. Ensure that all students understand the language of the scoring guide. As mentioned above, co-constructing scoring guides with students is one way to be sure that the guides use "student-friendly" language.

Key Takeaways

- The terms *scoring guide* and *rubric* are widely used interchangeably, but technically not all scoring guides are rubrics. A scoring guide is a rubric only when it includes three or more levels of quality.
- Scoring guides have become commonplace, but not all scoring guides are well written.
- There are two major types of scoring guides: holistic and analytical.
- Of the two types, holistic scoring guides are easier to write and score. They are preferred for summative tasks because they are not as specific as analytical scoring guides. Analytical scoring guides have an added level of specificity, making them useful for targeting feedback in conjunction with formative performance tasks.
- In developing a scoring guide, one option is to have all levels refer back to the Meets Success Criteria level; this avoids the need to write specific criteria for each level of the scoring guide.
- There are four types of feedback: task, process, self-regulation, and self (praise). Praise is the least effective kind of feedback, but it has its place in educational settings.
- Students can use scoring guides to conduct self- and peer assessment.
- When teacher and students co-construct scoring guides, students gain more ownership over their learning.

Reflection Questions

1. How do you use scoring guides in your classroom? How are teachers in your school or district using scoring guides?

2. Based on your current use of scoring guides, what changes do you think are necessary in scoring guide usage in your classroom, school, or district?

3. How would you rate the level of quality of the scoring guides used in your classroom, school, or district? What is good about the scoring guides? What needs to be improved?

4. Which of the four types of feedback do you think is predominant in your classroom? What type of feedback is lacking? How can you change that?

5. What resonated with you the most in this chapter and why?

7

Implementation Considerations

It is now time to consider the implementation of performance tasks in classrooms, schools, and/or districts, whether you have developed a performance task as you've been reading this book or not. Knowing how to develop a performance task is important, but the key to its impact on student learning is successful implementation. When you implement a performance task with your class, you need to take several factors into account, most of which are related to effective classroom instruction. If you are a school or district administrator and are considering implementation across your school or district, these factors need to be clearly communicated to staff members in that educational setting.

The first part of this chapter discusses a number of factors that influence the success of performance tasks in the classroom: student prior knowledge; teacher–student relationships; classroom management, with a focus on processes and procedures; and student grouping configurations for the completion of performance tasks. If these factors are not taken into consideration, the use of a performance task for learning or as an assessment will not result in deeper student engagement, motivation, and learning.

The second part of the chapter explores implementation options and provides some guidance on the implementation of performance tasks at the classroom, school, and district levels. Poor implementation has been the nemesis of success for many otherwise worthy initiatives over the years; the aim of this discussion is to help you avoid that fate for your performance tasks.

The overall intention of this chapter is to arm you with some instructional practices and strategies that will allow you to implement performance tasks with fidelity and reap the many benefits of the educational practices associated with performance tasks, furthering your development of assessment-capable learners.

Factors Influencing Performance Task Implementation

Student Prior Knowledge

It would be a crime to neglect the topic of student prior knowledge as an implementation consideration. Assessing student prior knowledge on instructional topics should be standard practice in every classroom. Students come to our classrooms with different levels of prior knowledge covering a wide range, from accurate knowledge about the focus of instruction to misconceptions about facts and concepts. Further, there are discrepancies among students in terms of skills.

Overwhelmingly, research has shown that a child's prior achievement is predictive of how that child will perform in current circumstances. These findings are consistent across ages, from the youngest learners through college and into careers. High achievers continue to be high achievers, and you know what happens with low achievers. John Hattie spoke on this topic at a conference I attended, and I can just hear him saying in his Kiwi accent, "Our job as teachers is to mess this up" (Hattie, 2012, p. 38). Teachers need to "mess up" the typical trajectory by "planning ways in which to accelerate the growth of those who start behind, so that they can most efficiently attain the curriculum and learning objectives of the lesson alongside the brightest students" (p. 38). The starting point is ascertaining what students already know, and this has to occur before you can plan your unit. A student's prior knowledge affects where he or she may start on a learning progression and/or on the SOLO learning intentions and accompanying success criteria. The SOLO learning intentions are incorporated into the performance task, and thus learning is scaffolded; with the right supports, student learning can be accelerated.

In addition to knowing what students already know and can do, teachers need to understand how students think. Hattie recommends revisiting one of the more tried-and-true theories of learning—Jean

Piaget's stages of learning. Do the sensorimotor, preoperational, concrete operational, and formal operational stages of learning ring any bells? You can do a quick search online to refresh your memory and find information on Piaget's learning theory. The message Hattie (2012) is trying to get across is that "we must know what students already know, know how they think, and then aim to progress all students towards the success criteria of the lesson" (p. 39). This is a tall order, but if you're up for it, using performance tasks that focus on the success criteria can help you mess up the typical trajectory and accelerate student learning.

About a week or two before you and your colleagues start planning an upcoming unit of instruction, you need to gather information on students' prior knowledge on the unit topic. This is the case even if you are not developing a performance task for the unit. For all units of instruction, you should be gathering some information on student prior knowledge before planning occurs. (For the most part, all of the instructional practices associated with performance tasks that are discussed in this book are practices that teachers should be doing on a daily basis.)

To assess students' prior knowledge, you have a few options, ranging from more formal to less formal. A more formal option would be to create a traditional pre-assessment with a few selected-response (multiple-choice, fill-in-the blank, matching) and a few constructed-response (short-response or extended-response) questions. It should not be too extensive—just long enough to provide you with evidence so you can make instructional planning decisions.

In his classroom in New Zealand, Steve Martin uses a number of more informal means to assess prior knowledge, many of which involve students working with partners or in small groups. In one such method, Martin writes one learning intention at each of the four levels for a primary standard. (This could result in a lot of learning intentions, depending how many priority standards you have, thus it is necessary to prioritize to write only a total of four.) He has students respond to the learning intentions individually in writing, then has small groups of students meet to share their responses. This allows the students to discuss their understandings and possibly clarify any misconceptions. This step could also be done with a whole-group discussion. Martin then provides an opportunity for students to ask questions on the upcoming topic, and he takes advantage of the student questions by incorporating them into lesson planning or by adjusting learning intentions that may have been utilized the previous year (Martin, 2011).

A tool that serves a similar purpose is the K-W-L chart, the name of which comes from *know* ("what I know"), *want* ("what I want to know"), and *learned* ("what I have learned"). You might pose an over-arching question about the topic and ask students to respond individually in the "know" section. This is an open enough approach that students may reveal a lot of information about their prior knowledge, including misconceptions that may need to be corrected. Students then move on to what they want to know about the topic. What are their burning questions? You could use the resulting questions in two ways: You might incorporate them into your planning of the unit learning intentions, as Martin does, and you could have students use them to establish their own learning goals for the unit. The "learned" component can be completed on the K-W-L chart or as part of the students' learning logs. What students learned does not have to match their questions. The K-W-L strategy could be done as a whole class or in small groups in which students individually complete the "know" section and then share with their team to clarify any misconceptions; the group could then collaboratively develop questions they would like answered.

Prior knowledge needs to be taken into consideration *before* unit planning occurs. The intent is to "mess up" the typical trajectory of students, accelerating those who are further behind so that *all* students can meet the success criteria. Performance tasks are your means of messing up the typical trajectory.

Teacher–Student Relationships

Teacher–student relationships are at the heart of student learning, as these relationships are connected to every part of the student learning process, including the introduction of performance tasks into instruction and assessment. It is no wonder that Hattie (2009) found teacher–student relationships to have an effect size of 0.72, which falls within the zone of desired effects. In *Classroom Management That Works*, Robert Marzano (2003) reports on research that revealed significant differences in effect size depending on the grade-level range. Marzano found an overall effect size of 0.76 for rules and procedures in regard to classroom management. The greatest impact was at the upper elementary and high school levels, with average effect sizes of 0.77; the effect size for middle school was 0.61. Classroom management clearly has a significant impact on student achievement.

The dynamics of the classroom climate, and thus the success of performance tasks, can be influenced greatly by teacher–student relationships. Teacher relationships with students, especially in the younger years, can be based on closeness or conflict. As John Hattie and Gregory Yates (2014) describe it, "Closeness refers to the emotional context of teaching interactions" (p. 17). Students whose relationships with you are based on closeness will seek you out in a time of need. In contrast, conflicts with students—and we've all had them—can make you want to leave teaching. Hattie and Yates present several findings in *Visible Learning and the Science of How We Learn* (2014) regarding the power of positive teacher–student relationships, including improvement of overall student well-being, diminishment of negativity students may feel about "adjusting and succeeding in school," and influence on students' likely life paths. These authors conclude: "The quality of teacher–student relationships can depend on how much time teachers interact with individual students in a non-coercive and friendly manner. A few minutes regularly listening to individual students can make a major difference in their lives" (p. 20).

Teacher–student relationships can have a lasting impact on students. Take a moment to reflect on the relationships you had with teachers when you were a student and those you have had with students as an educator. I know that I can name a handful of my own teachers from kindergarten through twelfth grade who had a lasting impact on me. If you think teacher–student relationships do not matter or do not truly have the large effect size indicated by the research, just read the following note, which I received from a former student after reconnecting with him on Facebook.

Thanks for the holiday wishes. I hope you enjoy your holidays with your family. I would absolutely love to share my experience with you. I'm in the process of putting the kids to bed so I will find time this weekend and email it to you.

I have been wanting to tell you how much of an impression you made on me when I was younger, so this is the perfect opportunity. Ever since I found you on Facebook, I have written my story down about you a thousand times, but the words never seem to fit the impact you had on me. Well, the kids are asleep so I guess I'll do it now.

As a kid all I ever wanted was for someone to take an interest in me and care about what I had to say. Growing up in NYC I moved around a lot and I never really had the opportunity to really feel comfortable in a classroom setting. Moving to Wellsville was no different. I felt like an outsider and I felt like I didn't belong, and I most certainly felt like I was not as smart as everyone else. I really felt like the teachers in Wellsville were

(Continued)

(Continued)

out of touch and uninterested in my needs. That may sound selfish but it's how I felt at the time. I had no desire to learn because I felt like I was pushed aside and uninspired.

Well, in comes Ms. Flach. You inspired me to learn and showed an interest in me that was never shown before. I felt like you looked past my defenses and saw a kid that wanted to learn and showed me that I actually mattered. You made me want to behave because I didn't want to let you down. You had faith and you believed in me, so I believed in you. I trusted that you were steering me in the right direction. I felt like Holden Caulfield from *Catcher in the Rye* at times. Everyone was a phony and you were the only genuine adult at the time. I remember you showing me pictures of your trip to Egypt and I remember thinking this lady is so cool. I want to travel and be like her.

You are one of a kind, truly special to me, and I have never forgotten you through the years. I will never forget how you inspired me and I can only hope that my kids will be lucky enough to have a teacher as amazing as you. I hope that all kids can experience their own "Ms. Flach." Not to go on and on but I've always wanted to make you proud, not just of me, but proud of yourself for having a part in who I am. So, thank you. Thank you for caring. Thank you for inspiring me. Thank you for showing me that I mattered. Thank you for giving me hope. Thank you for teaching me to be responsible for my own learning. As a side note, thanks for writing me and sending me pics when I went back to Brooklyn. My only regret is that my time as your student was too short. I'm glad that you sent me this message. It was really important for me to let you know how you have influenced my life.

Jerome Sanchez, Buffalo, NY

Deputy Sheriff

Erie County Sheriff's Department

If you were the teacher reading this Facebook message from a former student, would it not bring tears to your eyes? It certainly brought tears to mine. This is why we are teachers. Teachers can make a difference in the lives of students, even those students who have challenging backgrounds. Through good relationships, you can break down barriers and bring out the very best in your students, accelerating student learning. With strong teacher–student relationships, students are often willing to take on challenges they might otherwise have avoided, such as attempting the extended abstract levels of learning through the performance task.

A precise description of an "effective teacher" is elusive. To begin with, the word *effective* is subjective, and thus would not be suitable for use on a scoring guide. Interestingly, you are most likely able to distinguish an effective teacher from an ineffective teacher. In his book *Qualities of Effective Teachers,* James H. Stronge (2007) identifies a number of qualities from the research (qualities over which teachers have control) that positively influence teachers' impact on student achievement. Stronge does not specifically address teacher–student relationships, but these relationships are evident in his chapter titled "The Teacher as a Person," in which he discusses "interview and survey responses about effective teaching" that "emphasize the teacher's affective characteristics, or social and emotional behaviors, more than pedagogical practice" (p. 22). The issue is the ability to quantify affective "characteristics such as a love of children, a love of work, and positive relationships with colleagues and children" (p. 22). Hattie presents similar findings in *Visible Learning* (2009): "When students, parents, principals, and teachers were asked about what influences students' achievement, all but the teachers emphasized the relationships between teachers and students" (p. 118). The process of a teacher's developing a relationship with a student "implies agency, efficacy, respect by the teacher for what the child brings to the class (from home, culture, peers), and allowing the experiences of the child to be recognized in the classroom" (p. 118). Teachers need the skills of "listening, empathy, caring, and having a positive regard for others" (p. 118) in order to develop meaningful relationships with students. These skills are also evident in effective teachers. Specifically, effective teachers "practice focused and sympathetic listening to show students they care not only about what happens in the classroom but about students' lives in general. These teachers initiate two-way communication that exudes trust, tact, honesty, humility, and care" (Stronge, 2007, p. 23).

Effective teachers are aware of their students' interests both in school and outside school. According to Stronge (2007), what differentiates good teachers from effective teachers is that "effective teachers care for students first as people, and second as students" (p. 24). In their book *Student Voice,* Russ Quaglia and Michael Corso (2014) take this idea a

Effect Sizes	
Teacher–student relationships	0.72
Teacher clarity	0.75
Feedback	0.73

step further. Their "Aspirations Profile" identifies four quadrants, with high and low future/dreaming on the *y*-axis and high and low present/doing on the *x*-axis. Students typically fall into one of these four quadrants. If a student is low on both future/dreaming and present/doing, he or she is said to be in a state of "hibernation." A student in hibernation "has no goals for the future and puts in no effort in the present." A student high in future/dreaming is in the state of "imagination." A student in this state "sets goals for the future but does not put forth effort to reach those goals." A student low on future/dreaming but high on present/doing is in a state of "perspiration." This student "works hard in the present, but has no goals for the future." The final quadrant of high future/dreaming and high present/doing is "aspiration." A student in this state "sets goals for the future and puts forth effort in the present to reach those goals" (p. 15). Just asking students to think about their future and what they might want to do can go a long way in teacher–student relationships, but the benefit is greater than that—such interest from teachers brings students into the learning process. I remember a seventh-grade remedial reading student, Ricky. Living in Oswego, New York, he grew up an avid hockey player and fan. He wanted to be a professional hockey player. This student was high on his future dreams and was also high on his present/doing as he was on the local hockey travel team, having started skating as a toddler. I had made a connection with Ricky by finding out about his interests outside school. I also remember other students, in particular Ian, who could be challenging to make connections with. If I had just asked Ian what he was interested in, or what he wanted to be when he grew up, perhaps I could have awoken him from "hibernation." The creation of positive teacher–student relationships is closely related to the work on student voice, and I highly encourage you to learn more about this work if you are truly interested in creating a collaborative learning environment with actively engaged students in all phases.

Using equitable and positive classroom behaviors is another way in which teachers can promote an appropriate level of student cooperation. Such teacher behaviors include making eye contact with all students when addressing the class, rather than focusing on only a few or those in the front of the room; roaming around the room to ensure that all students are in close proximity at some point during the instructional period and all students are acknowledged; and ensuring that all students have the ability to participate in conversations and activities. To ensure that all students get to discuss how they would solve a math problem, you might try doing a think-pair-share instead of asking one student to demonstrate solving the problem on the board. Consider asking a colleague or administrator to visit your classroom to observe and give you feedback on the level of equity you display when asking questions or the level of active participation in your class. Make sure that when you are asking questions you allow the same amount of wait time for all students, no matter their level of ability or past performance.

Teacher–student relationships play a critical role in the learning process. They can have either positive or negative impacts on students and thus on how students do on performance tasks, as well as how they behave during performance tasks. Positive relationships with students are such an important aspect of teaching that Hattie (2012) identifies developing those relationships as one of his original eight "mind frames": "Mind frame 7: Teachers/leaders believe that it is their role to develop positive relationships in classroom/staffrooms" (p. 165). This mind frame reminds us that the classroom climate needs to exude warmth, trustworthiness, and empathy, and the teacher is responsible for creating such a climate. Students need to have a level of comfort in the classroom so that they can take risks and ask questions when they don't know, or respond to questions without fear of being ridiculed. All of these activities take place during the implementation of performance tasks. Students need to be able to trust that the classroom climate is one in which their errors and mistakes are seen as learning opportunities, and that the classroom is a safe haven for learning (Hattie, 2012). Teacher–student relationships can thrive in a classroom where the teacher ensures that students feel safe, respected, and cared for, all for the sake of deep learning through performance tasks.

Classroom Management: Rules and Processes

It seems appropriate to move into a discussion of classroom management after addressing teacher–student relationships, since the two are closely connected. Performance tasks can be a challenge to implement if classroom management is not strong. There are many components to classroom management, all of which are important in the development of an effective classroom that promotes student learning and the successful implementation of performance tasks. The area of classroom management that is most important to the implementation of performance tasks, however, is the establishment of rules and procedures, with an emphasis on procedures. Overall, classroom management has an effect size of 0.52, but the research on classroom management reveals that the effect size for rules and procedures is 0.76 (Hattie, 2009). Different aspects of classroom management have varying degrees of effectiveness.

> An effectively managed classroom is one that runs smoothly, with minimal confusion and downtime, and maximizes opportunities for student learning. An effective classroom has patterns and routines in place that make interaction and movement easy to organize and accomplish. (Evertson, Emmer, & Worsham, 2006, p. 20)

A classroom that runs like a well-oiled machine optimizes the use of time, materials, and space to promote learning for all students. The tools that can help you create such a classroom are the rules and procedures that facilitate the learning process, especially during the implementation of performance tasks.

Rules and Procedures

Both rules and procedures are expectations for specified behaviors. Rules tend to be general expectations about behaviors, whereas procedures are expectations for the manner of accomplishing tasks (Emmer, Evertson, & Worsham, 2006; Evertson et al., 2006). The rules and procedures established in a classroom should be intended to be used from the first day of school to the last day of school.

Whether you develop the rules and procedures collaboratively with students or not, you need to take three actions to ensure that the rules and procedures are understood and followed. First, you need to communicate to the students what the rules and procedures are, and not just by posting them or requiring that they be memorized. Students need to know exactly what the rules and procedures mean and why they are in place. You should have classroom discussions on the rules, giving examples and explaining why each rule is important to have in the classroom.

Second, you need to give students the opportunity to practice the rules and procedures. When it comes to the rules, which focus on expected behaviors such as "respecting others and property," students generally should be able to follow them once you have clarified their meaning and importance. In the case of the procedures, however, students will often have the need for physical practice, especially at the elementary level. Practicing such procedures as lining up to go to lunch is not necessary at the secondary level, but students at this level do need to be instructed in some procedures, such as what they should do when returning to class after an absence. The goal of having set procedures is to maximize the use of instructional time and limit the amount of downtime. In the case of high school students returning after absences, it should be enough for you simply to communicate that information from the previous day's lesson is available in a binder or folder kept on the bookshelf at the back of the room. If you plan to have students give and receive peer feedback, you will need to teach the related procedures directly at the elementary level and possibly at the middle school level, depending on how much exposure the students have had to peer feedback. After teaching students how to give and receive feedback to a peer using the scoring guide, you might have them physically practice with partners using a writing prompt that has been completed with an accompanying scoring guide. As part of teaching students how to give feedback using a scoring guide, you should model desirable behaviors with a student. As students progress through middle and high school, their need to practice procedures diminishes.

Finally, you need to address with students what will happen if they do not follow the rules and procedures that have been established. If you want to have effective rules and procedures, you must teach them, practice them, and act on them.

At the elementary level, procedures can be divided into six categories: procedures for room areas, procedures for seatwork and teacher-led activities, procedures for transitions into and out of the room, procedures for small-group work, procedures for cooperative group activities, and general procedures (Evertson et al., 2006). At the secondary level there are four categories: general procedures needed for each class period, procedures for teacher-led instruction and seatwork activities, procedures for group work, and miscellaneous procedures (Emmer et al., 2006). Some of the differences between the elementary and secondary categories are a result of the fact that most elementary classrooms are self-contained, with students starting and ending the school day in the same classroom, as compared to both middle and high schools, in which the day is organized into a set number of instructional segments, each designated for a different content area or lunch.

The two categories of procedures that are pertinent to performance tasks at the elementary level are procedures for seatwork and teacher-led activities and procedures for cooperative group activities. To some extent, procedures for small-group work may be applicable during performance tasks. At the secondary level, the procedure categories most applicable to performance tasks are procedures for teacher-led instruction and seatwork activities and procedures for group work. The following sections discuss the pertinent categories and how these procedures might be applicable while students are completing a performance task.

Seatwork and Teacher-Led Activities/Teacher-Led Instruction and Seatwork

These two categories contain some common procedures that are applicable during performance tasks, the first of which concern student attention during presentations. The procedure looks a bit different at the elementary level than it does at the secondary level, but the overall intention is to make clear what behaviors are expected of students while they are watching an adult or a peer at the front of the class providing instruction or sharing a performance task presentation. Even if the performance task is the learning vehicle, an instructional component of some kind is needed in order for students to apply learning to complete the task. For example, if elementary students are learning to write an opinion piece and the on-demand preassessment has revealed that the students struggle with establishing an organizational structure for their reasons, they will need a minilesson addressing organizational structures. High school students in an Earth science class are going to need surface-level knowledge so they have something to relate to and extend as they complete their performance task. In either of these cases, as the teacher is presenting, what are students expected to do? There could be a specific procedure in place, such as for mini-lessons during elementary writing instruction: Take out your writing journal; turn to the mini-lesson section; write in the date and topic; take notes on key points as directed. In Earth science, as the teacher presents the information included on a weather map, students maybe expected to take notes using the Cornell system (a great tool that challenges students to summarize the information in their notes).

If a student is giving a performance task presentation in front of the class, whether at the elementary or the secondary level, the other students should be able to use the scoring guide to organize feedback to be given to the presenting student later. There may be specific procedures, depending on the presentation. For instance, if a small group of students have written and are presenting a play, most likely it would not be appropriate for the observing students to ask questions. However, if the presentation is on climate change, it may be an expectation that each of the observing students will write down two questions during the presentation to seek clarification at the end of the presentation.

There are two procedures at both levels that in my mind go together. The first concerns student talking, and the second concerns the teacher's method for gaining student attention (Emmer et al., 2006; Evertson et al., 2006). Talking is inevitable as students are completing performance tasks (unless the tasks are summative), as you will be encouraging students and teaching them how to provide peer feedback using the scoring guides. You may need to establish a procedure for peer feedback—not just how to give and receive peer feedback, but how students are to pair up (does each have one particular partner, or do students sign up to get partners when they need feedback?). It may be necessary to put a procedure in place to gain everyone's attention, at either level. If students are all working with partners and you need to get the whole class's attention to provide some clarifying information, you could use a sound, such as a bell or ringing chimes. At the elementary level students love repeat clapping patterns, or responding in chorus to a phrase such as *Red Robin . . . (Yumm)* (Tate, 2014). Any of these methods, as long as it is taught and practiced (and failures to practice it are acted upon), can be used to bring students to silence and gain their attention. You determine what behavior is expected when you ring a bell, clap, or speak a certain phrase.

The final procedure that needs to be established, at both levels, concerns what students are to do when they have completed their performance tasks. The two givens when a performance task is completed should be self- and peer evaluation against the scoring guide and the making of adjustments based on the feedback. Students should first self-assess their work and make adjustments before seeking peer feedback. Once they have made necessary adjustments to their performance tasks, they can arrange for peer feedback. So, what procedure should students use to get peer feedback? Remember, any procedure can be changed if it is not working, but if you don't have one in place to begin with, students will have to figure out on their own what to do to get peer feedback. Also, since students will finish both self- and peer evaluations at different times, the big question becomes, what do students do when they are finished? If you intend to use learning logs, this would be a great opportunity for students to reflect on the learning intentions and success criteria. Depending on the success criteria and if the performance task is a presentation, such reflection may need to be completed after the actual presentation.

Here is a possible procedure for students who are completing a formative performance task prior to, say, a more traditional assessment with multiple-choice, short-response, and extended-response questions. As students complete the performance task, they sign up in a presentation group of four or five students. If there are five students in the group, each student would have four scoring guides. If, for instance, each student has created a political cartoon for a U.S. history class that will be included in a class book, each student in the group would pass his or her cartoon to the person on the right, who would then evaluate it against the scoring guide. When that evaluation is completed, the cartoons would be passed to the right again, until each person has completed four scoring guides with feedback for the other students. If students need to present their performance task, they could also do so in small groups following the same proce-dure. Students just need to be aware of the procedures and have the appropriate scoring guides.

Procedures for Cooperative Group Activities/ Procedures for Group Work

This section focuses on classroom procedures associated with cooperative group work, and not necessarily on group work as an instructional strategy. Several procedures and routines for coopera-tive learning groups are applicable to both elementary and secondary classrooms. The following recommendations come from the work of Edmund T. Emmer, Carolyn M. Evertson, and Murray E. Worsham, in particular their books *Classroom Management for Elementary Teachers* (Evertson et al., 2006) and *Classroom Management for Middle and High School Teachers* (Emmer et al., 2006). Each of these books includes a chapter devoted entirely to specific strategies for managing coopera-tive learning groups. The following list is just the tip of the iceberg:

1. *Room arrangement:* If students are going to work in cooperative or small learning groups, their desks or tables should be arranged into small groups. The groups should be spaced far enough apart to allow easy walking paths and to ensure that students are not distracted by the conversations of other groups.

2. *Talk and movement procedures:* It is natural for noise levels to increase when you first start using groups, so you need to establish expectations for both talk and movement. For instance, remind students not to talk over each other; one per-son should be allowed to finish speaking before another one speaks. Assigning roles for the group members is a means of holding all student accountable; one of these roles could be "materials manager," the person responsible for obtaining the materials needed for the performance task.

3. *Group attention signals:* As students are working in their groups, you may need to interrupt them occasionally to pro-vide clarification of directions or to correct misconceptions you have been hearing while monitoring the groups. Prear-range with students what type of signal or cue you will use to indicate that they should stop talking, stop doing whatever they are doing, and focus their attention on you.

4. *Promotion of interdependence:* Emphasize for students that in group work, individual success is connected to the success of all the members of the group. You might use the metaphor of a jigsaw puzzle, in which the whole is made up of many pieces. Each person becomes an expert in one aspect of the performance task, and then the experts share their respective components to create the final product (Frey, Fisher, & Everlove, 2009).

5. *Individual accountability:* If each student is completing his or her own performance task, but with group support, individual accountability does not become an issue. Questions of individual accountability arise when everyone in the group gets the same grade on the group product and some members did not contribute as much as others. If some students appear to be contributing minimally to the group product, consider adding a component that students must complete individually.

6. *Effective group work skills:* Individuals in a group need three main types of skills in order for their group to be effective: social skills, explaining skills, and leadership skills. Students need direct instruction in these skills, as well as practice and feedback. The social skills needed for group work include active listening, sharing, and supporting. Explaining skills are associated with the performance task and accomplishing the task; students with good explaining skills are solid with the surface level of understanding. Group interactions on the learning may focus on each person writing one question on the content that needs clarifying, followed by the group helping to explain the content associated with the questions. Leadership skills are demonstrated by team members who step up and plan how to approach the performance task, or who encourage other members to complete their portion of the performance task and support their learning when necessary.

7. *Formation of groups:* When students are to engage in group work, you need to consider how the groups should be formed. As much as students should be able to work with anyone in a group, it is sometimes appropriate to separate certain students from each other. Aim to have a range of academic abilities in each group, as well as someone who is a potential leader who will step up and support the team.

It seems appropriate to end the above list with the formation of groups given that the next, very brief, section is on student grouping considerations. The bottom line on classroom management is that when you do it well, your classroom will run like a well-oiled machine, and when you do it poorly, your classroom will come to a grinding halt, and you will find that implementing performance tasks becomes too challenging. As a former administrator once said to me, "If you take care of the little things, you won't have to deal with the big things." Establish strong classroom management practices, and you will not have behavior problems that disrupt instructional time.

Student Grouping Considerations

The final factor influencing performance task implementation is whether students will be working in groups or individually to complete the performance task or series of performance tasks within the unit. The performance task itself may drive your decision on this point: For certain performance tasks, you may want individual accountability; for others, it might be useful to have students work with partners or in small groups of three or four.

Your organization of students may also be based on how the performance task is being used. If students are completing the task as a summative assessment in which they will receive a grade, then they should work individually. If the performance task is formative, you can use whatever grouping you like. Another factor that you might consider is how challenging and how comprehensive the performance task is. For example, a high school civics performance task that includes a number of components is being completed as a learning experience and will be followed up with a traditional unit assessment. In such a case, with the performance task being used as a learning experience, having students be able to converse and process their understanding as they are developing different components of the performance task is an instructional "win." You could have students complete the performance task as a cooperative learning group. One component of cooperative learning groups is positive interdependence—that is, individual success is dependent on the success of everyone else in the group. Accordingly, "the structure of the task must demand that each member of the group offer a unique contribution to the joint effort. When students perceive that every member is indispensable to achieving their mutual goals and that they are both dependent on and obligated to their peers, conditions are ripe for collaborative learning" (Frey et al., 2009, p. 23).

Since peer assessment is a valuable practice for providing students with feedback, students should be partnered with peers for this purpose. As mentioned previously, you should instruct students on how to give and receive peer feedback, making expectations clear and providing opportunity for practice.

There are a variety of ways you can organize students to complete performance tasks. The two main considerations are how the performance task is being used (formatively or summatively) and how challenging and comprehensive the performance task is. There is power in processing understanding to deepen that understanding, which can be accomplished in small groups. The success of any student configuration used for performance tasks is dependent on how the tasks are organized and structured for effectiveness.

Implementation Options

Appendix 8 contains a template for an implementation success action plan (also available on this book's page at the Corwin website: http://www.corwin.com/books/Book249034). No matter where you are implementing performance tasks—at whatever grade level, in classroom, department, school, or district—you can use this plan to enhance implementation fidelity.

As mentioned at the start of this chapter, the success of many initiatives has been hampered by poor implementation. The "knowing-doing gap" has become a recognized phenomenon in the business world, thanks to Jeffrey Pfeffer and Robert Sutton's book *The Knowing-Doing Gap: How Smart Companies Turn Knowledge Into Action* (2000). You could say that the field of education suffers from an implementation gap. We have a tendency to focus so much on the "what" that we forget about the most important aspect, the "how" (Barber, Rodriguez, & Artis, 2016). The implementation success action plan should be considered a living document—including reflections, adjustments in action steps, and data (qualitative and quantitative) gathered through regular monitoring until performance tasks become the "norm" in your classroom, grade level, department, school, or district.

Principles of Change

As you create your implementation success action plan, keep in mind the 10 principles of change articulated by Gene Hall and Shirley Hord in *Implementing Change: Patterns, Principles, and Potholes* (2011), which are summarized below. These are all worthy principles, but some may be more pertinent to your plan than others, depending on the position you hold and the extent of the performance task implementation you hope to achieve.

Change Principle 1: Change is learning—it's as simple and as complicated as that.

Summary: When change is introduced, in this case the implementation of performance tasks, professional development needs to accompany the change, as instructional staff need to know how to create and implement performance tasks. Just knowing is not necessarily enough; modeling and feedback are also important for successful implementation.

Change Principle 2: Change is a process, not an event.

Summary: Do not expect a book study or a two-day professional development session to result in deep implementation of performance tasks with fidelity to the process and instructional practices embedded. In planning for change, expect a three- to five-year process for deep implementation with fidelity, including all the resources, professional development, and coaching necessary to support implementation.

Change Principle 3: The school is the primary unit for change.

Summary: The school instructional and administrative staff can act as the "engine that could" or the engine that failed. To be the "engine that could," the staff requires the support of others within and outside the system. The needs of each school must be taken into consideration, as implementation is not a one-size-fits-all process. The power to succeed in the implementation of a new initiative lies within the school. For the building leaders reading this book, know that your school could be leading the charge for utilizing performance tasks in the classroom, but you need support from the district and from outside facilitators.

Change Principle 4: Organizations adopt change—individuals implement change.

Summary: As Hall and Hord (2011) state succinctly, "An entire organization does not change until each member has changed" (p. 9). Even if an organization, such as a district, implements the use of performance tasks in classroom instruction, some individuals will jump on board immediately, others will take their time getting on, and still others will let the boat sail without them. For implementation to be successful, meaning that practice has changed and student outcomes have been improved, everyone needs to cross the "implementation bridge." As staff learn, they can begin to change their practices, but they need support to cross the bridge and not fall into the chasm below.

Change Principle 5: Interventions are key to the success of the change process.

Summary: Think of interventions as "touchpoints." Hall and Hord (2011) refer to brief interventions as "one-legged interviews"; for example, a principal touches base with a teacher on the way to a meeting and plants the seed, "How are you doing planning your performance task?" The more touchpoints that occur, the better, as the initiative is not going away, and it is being brought to the forefront with each touchpoint.

Change Principle 6: Appropriate interventions reduce resistance to change.

Summary: Some people will resist the change to using more performance tasks, and it is necessary to determine the reasons for their resistance. People's resistance to change usually stems from one of three causes: (1) They don't want to leave their comfort zones; (2) they question the validity of the change, such as whether performance tasks can make a difference; or (3) change is just hard for them—for some people, change can be downright painful. See Hall and Hord's (2011) book for suggestions of different kinds of interventions you might use to deal with each of these reasons for resistance.

Change Principle 7: Administrator leadership is essential to long-term change success.

Summary: A change cannot sustain itself over the long run if "administrators do not engage in ongoing active support" (Hall & Hord, 2011, p. 14). Administrators need to attend the professional development sessions, provide "touchpoints" at every opportunity each day, obtain the necessary resources, and build the foundation that will sustain the change. Building and district administrators, this applies to you specifically. What delivery structures can you put in place as part of your implementation success action plan?

Change Principle 8: Facilitating change is a team effort.

Summary: Facilitating change is an ongoing effort, and not just on the part of one or a few people—a team needs to spearhead the implementation of performance tasks. In *Deliverology in Practice: How Education Leaders Are Improving Student Outcomes,* Barber et al. (2016) describe the "Delivery Unit," which is "a person or team responsible for driving the achievement of your aspiration, no matter what. Led by your delivery leader, the Delivery Unit is the one group in your system that you can count on to be immune to distractions, even when you yourself have to respond to them" (p. 45). Who is part of your delivery unit, the guiding force that will keep performance tasks on the radar screen no matter what?

Change Principle 9: Mandates can work.

Summary: Mandates have gotten a bad name, but the use of mandates can actually be a good strategy to support implementation. A mandate makes the expectation for the implementation clear, but to be successful it needs to be "accompanied by continuing communication, ongoing learning, on-site coaching, and time for implementation" (Hall & Hord, 2011, p. 15).

Change Principle 10: The context influences the process of learning and change.

Summary: Since the school is the main unit for change, certain school characteristics can have strong impacts on change efforts. First, the school's physical features, such as the size and layout of the buildings, as well as its available resources, present policies, and staff procedures can influence implementation success. Second, people factors are important, such as the attitudes, beliefs, and values of those involved in the change. A collaborative culture among staff members who value the establishment of common goals for improvement can be accepting of change, whereas a culture with a top-down approach can be detrimental to change. What kind of culture exists in your building or district?

Of course, there are many different ways to approach the implementation of performance tasks. The information below is intended to guide your thinking. I will not attempt to suggest a specific implementation plan because too many variables would need to be taken into consideration. Appendix 5 provides guidelines for completing an implementation success action plan, and Appendix 6 offers an example of such a plan. Each teacher, building, and district will have its own plan, and even within a district, buildings might have different implementation success action plans, because each has its own needs and personalities. As you develop your implementation plan, remember to try to approach change as a process and not an event. Be the tortoise, not the hare—strive for slow and steady progress.

Below are a few suggestions for the implementation of performance tasks, depending on your position.

Classroom Teacher

- Aim to try one performance task in the next two months. That will give you time to plan it, prepare for it, and utilize it. After you administer the performance task, reflect on what was successful and make adjustments to the performance task as needed so you can use it again next year. If students produced written products, make copies of those that meet the success criteria, or take pictures if physical products were created. The point is to gather samples that you can use in future years to involve students by having them co-construct scoring guides and or/success criteria.
- Set goals as to how many performance tasks you would like to complete by the end of your present school year and use your implementation success action plan to map out the steps you need to take to achieve your goal.

Building Administrator

- Form a small team of people who become champions for change. Work with the team to develop the implementation success action plan through a collaborative effort.

District Administrator

- Select a small group of building administrators who can become champions for change and lead their buildings to successful deep implementation of performance tasks, with fidelity, over the next three to five years.
- Ensure that each of these buildings has the resources it needs. Remember, one size does not fit all.
- Enlist other district administrators and, in conjunction with the targeted building administrators, develop a district-wide implementation success action plan.

Implementation can be the downfall of performance tasks for a number of different reasons, and it is essential that you take all of these into consideration when you venture into creating and implementing performance tasks in your classroom, school, or district. Don't let your hard work in creating a performance task be derailed by poor classroom management or by failure to assess student prior knowledge before planning. By using an implementation success action plan to ensure that you take the steps necessary to address the considerations described in this chapter, you can successfully implement performance tasks to move students to deeper levels of understanding.

Key Takeaways

- Poor implementation has been the nemesis of success for many initiatives, often as a result of too much time spent on the "what" and not enough spent on the "how."
- Student prior knowledge should be assessed before planning for instruction and assessment occurs.
- Positive teacher–student relationships can have lasting impacts on students.
- Teachers need to develop classroom climates that exude warmth, trustworthiness, and empathy so students feel safe to make mistakes and see errors as learning opportunities.
- Classroom rules and procedures go hand in hand with good teacher–student relationships.
- When it comes to procedures and general expectations, remember to teach them, practice them, and act on them.
- Teaching classroom rules and procedures is important at all levels; practicing procedures is important in elementary school and sometimes in middle school; acting on student failure to follow rules and procedures needs to occur at every level.
- Cooperative group activities are beneficial, but they must be well planned to be effective.
- Performance tasks can be completed in a variety of student configurations. Just take into consideration whether the task is summative or formative and how comprehensive it is.
- Hall and Hord (2011) detail 10 principles of change that need to be taken into consideration in the implementation of a new initiative.
- The implementation success action plan is a tool to guide implementation at any level, from the classroom to the district.

Reflection Questions

1. How does assessing student prior knowledge benefit instructional planning and assessment?

2. If you are a teacher, how would you describe the teacher–student relationships in your present classroom? If you are an administrator, what do you notice in your building or district about teacher–student relationships? Are there any supports or actions you could put in place to help teachers build better relationships with students?

3. What are your takeaways from this chapter's section on classroom management?

4. What is your level of understanding of cooperative learning groups? Have you used true cooperative learning groups? If so, what benefits did you see as a result?

5. Which of the 10 principles of change listed in this chapter do you view as the most challenging and why?

6. What are your current intentions for implementation of performance tasks?

7. What resonated with you the most in this chapter and why?

Appendix 1

Unit Planning Template: Performance Task

Teacher(s)/Team: Michelle Caulk, Monica McCurry, Emily Peterson

Grade Level: Third

Unit Title/Type (topical, thematic, skills-based): Narrative Analysis and Opinion Writing

Step 1. Identify the Primary Standards and Secondary Standards.

Unit Primary Standards

W.3.1 Write opinion pieces on topics or texts, supporting a point of view with reasons.

   a. Introduce the topic or text they are writing about, state an opinion, and create an organizational structure that lists reasons.

   b. Provide reasons that support the opinion.

   c. Use linking words and phrases (e.g., *because, therefore, since, for example*) to connect opinion and reasons.

   d. Provide a concluding statement or section.

Unit Secondary Standards

L.RI.3.7 Use information gained from illustrations (e.g., maps, photographs) and the words in a text to demonstrate understanding of the text (e.g., where, when, why, and how key events occur).

L.RI.3.10 By the end of the year, read and comprehend informational texts, including history/social studies, science, and technical texts, at the high end of the grades 2–3 text complexity band independently and proficiently.

Step 2. Learning Progressions: What do you need to teach first? What follows? What comes next, etcetera? This includes subskills and enabling knowledge that is needed to attain the skills and knowledge within the standard, which are the end of the learning progression. Identify the understandings, etc.

W.3.1 Write opinion pieces on topics or texts, supporting a point of view with reasons.

		Subskills and Skills	Enabling Knowledge (information, facts) and Concepts
	Learning Progression ↓	Define	Opinion or stance
		Differentiate	Convincing versus nonconvincing reasons to support your opinion
		Identify	Evidence that supports reasons
		List	Components of an opinion introduction
		List	Linking words associated with opinion writing
		List	Components of an opinion conclusion
Understandings: "This is important to learn because . . ."		Writing opinion pieces are to convey your point of view in an attempt to change one's perspective, belief, or call them to action	
		A clear organization when writing your opinion more convincing	

SOLO Level	Unistructural: One Idea	Multistructural: Many Ideas; No Connections Between Facts and Ideas	Relational: Connections Between Facts and Ideas	Extended Abstract: Generalize Learning and Apply to Different Contexts	
Student-friendly learning intention: "We are learning to . . ."	Write opinion pieces on topics or texts and support your opinions with reasons. Write an introduction and conclusion for an opinion writing piece. Use opinion linking words to connect reasons. Organize stance, reasons, and supporting details in a structure that develops an opinion piece.				
SOLO Verbs	Define	List/compare	Justify	Create	Connect
Success criteria: "We are successful when we are able to . . ."	Opinion	Reasons (differentiate) to support your opinion	Each reason for your opinion with supporting details, keeping the audience in mind	An opinion piece on a topic with an introduction describing the topic and your stance on the topic with reasons and a conclusion using linking words	
	Stance	Components of an opinion introduction and conclusion			
		Linking words for opinion writing			
Context for learning: "Students will engage in their learning by . . ."	Reading two sources about influential African Americans, developing a stance on which African American should be the representative for the school display case, and creating a five-paragraph writing piece using both sources				

First Attempt

Performance Task

Performance Task Basics

Authentic task: Contest

Role/position: Student/third-grade student

Audience: Principal

Motivating context: Famous African Americans represented in school display case

Performance Task Student Description

In honor of Black History Month, Dr. Frampton (school principal) would like your opinion of who should be honored in the school's display case. Write a letter telling her about an influential African American and why that person should be honored.

Exceeds Success Criteria	Meets Success Criteria	Approaching Meets Success Criteria	A Long Way From Meets Success Criteria
Everything in Meets Success Criteria, Plus: • Includes quoted examples. • More than 3 reasons are given.	• Opinion is stated. • 3 reasons for opinion are listed. • Reasons are supported with evidence from sources. • Opinion linking words and phrases are used to connect reasons and evidence. • Components of an opinion introduction are included. • Components of an opinion conclusion are included.	• At least 4 of 6 Meets Success Criteria have been attained.	• 1–3 of Meets Success Criteria have been attained.

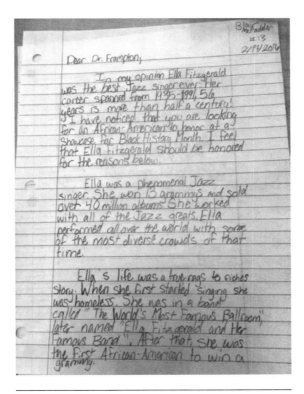

Source: Blair 1

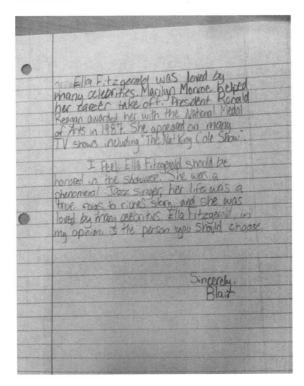

Source: Blair 2

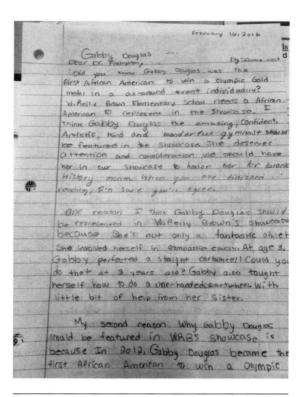

Source: Emma 1

Source: Emma 2

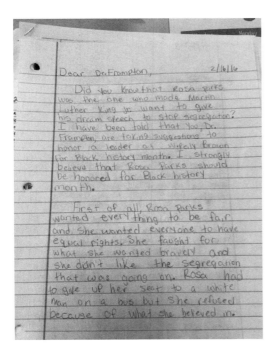

Dear Dr. Frampton,   2/16/16

Did you know that Rosa Parks was the one who made Martin Luther King Jr. want to give his dream speech to stop segregation? I have been told that you, Dr. Frampton, are taking suggestions to honor a leader at Wopely Brown for Black history month. I strongly believe that Rosa Parks should be honored for Black history month.

First of all, Rosa Parks wanted everything to be fair and she wanted everyone to have equal rights. She fought for what she wanted bravely and she didn't like the segregation that was going on. Rosa had to give up her seat to a white man on a bus but she refused because of what she believed in.

Source: Jayda 1

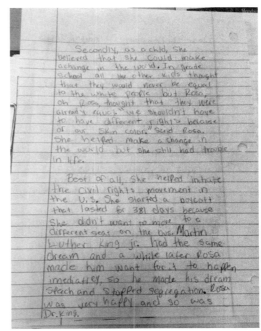

Secondly, as a child, she believed that she could make a change in the world. In grade school all the other kids thought that they would never be equal to the white people but Rosa, oh Rosa, thought that they were already equal. "We shouldn't have to have different rights because of our skin color." Said Rosa. She helped make a change in the world but she still had trouble in life.

Best of all, she helped initiate the civil rights movement in the U.S. She started a boycott that lasted for 381 days because she didn't want to move to a different seat on the bus. Martin Luther King Jr. had the same dream and a while later Rosa made him want for it to happen immediately, so he made his dream speech and stopped segregation. Rosa was very happy and so was Dr. King.

Source: Jayda 2

I believe Rosa Parks should be honored for black history month for the three main reasons you just heard. She wanted everything to be fair, as a child she believed that she could make a change in the world, and best of all, she helped initiate the civil rights movement in the U.S. Without Rosa Parks, we might still of had segregation because she made Dr. King want to make that speech. ROSA PARKS FOREVER!

Sincerely,
Jayda Johnson

Source: Jayda 3

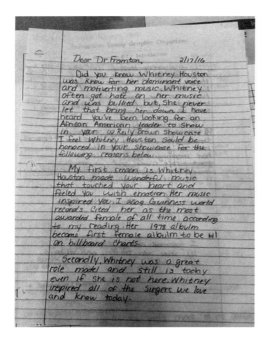

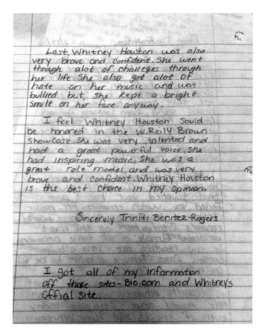

Source: Triniti 1

Source: Triniti 2

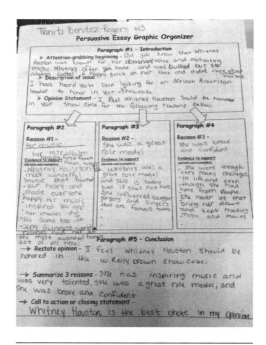

Source: Triniti 3

Appendix 2

Unit Planning Templates: Examples for Grades 3 and 11

Grade 3 Unit Planning Example

Teacher(s)/Team: Sample
Grade Level: Third
Unit Title/Type (topical, thematic, skills-based): Narrative Analysis and Opinion Writing
Step 1. Identify the Primary Standards and Secondary Standards.

Unit Primary Standards

RL.3.2 Recount stories, ~~including fables, folktales, and myths~~ from diverse cultures; determine the central message, ~~lesson, or moral~~ and explain how it is conveyed through key details in the text.

RL.3.3 Describe characters in a story (e.g., their traits, motivations, or feelings) and explain how their actions contribute to the sequence of events.

W.3.1 Write opinion pieces on topics or texts, supporting a point of view with reasons.

    a. Introduce the topic or text they are writing about, state an opinion, and create an organizational structure that lists reasons.

    b. Provide reasons that support the opinion.

   c. Use linking words and phrases (e.g., *because, therefore, since, for example*) to connect opinion and reasons.

   d. Provide a concluding statement or section.

Unit Secondary Standards

RL.3.1 Ask and answer questions to demonstrate understanding of a text, referring explicitly to the text as the basis for the answers.

L.3.1 Demonstrate command of the conventions of standard English grammar and usage when writing or speaking.

   e. Form and use the simple (e.g., *I walked; I walk; I will walk)* verb tenses.

   f. Ensure subject–verb and pronoun–antecedent agreement.

   g. Produce simple, compound, and complex sentences.

Step 2. Learning Progressions: What do you need to teach first? What follows? What comes next? This includes subskills and enabling knowledge that is needed to attain the skills and knowledge within the standard, which are the end of the learning progression. Identify the understandings, etc.

RL.3.2 Recount stories, ~~including fables, folktales, and myths~~ from diverse cultures; determine the central message, ~~lesson, or moral~~ and explain how it is conveyed through key details in the text.

	Subskills and Skills	Enabling Knowledge (information, facts) and Concepts
	Differentiate	Relevant and irrelevant details
	Identify	The central message
	Identify	Relevant details in relation to the central message
	Determine	Time order of key events
	Recount (retell)	Story
Understandings: "This is important to learn because . . ."	Stories are written to communicate key messages.	
	Authors include details to clearly communicate their key messages.	
	Stories are written with a key message and several supporting messages.	

Learning Progression (label along vertical axis of table)

Step 3. Write SOLO Learning Intentions and Success Criteria

SOLO Level	Unistructural: One Idea	Multistructural: Many Ideas; No Connections Between Facts and Ideas	Relational: Connections Between Facts and Ideas	Extended Abstract: Generalize Learning and Apply to Different Contexts
Student-friendly learning intention: "We are learning to . . ."	Retell stories from different cultures and be able to state the central messages of the stories along with details from the stories to support the messages.			
SOLO Verbs	Identify	List	Explain	Evaluate
Success criteria: "We are successful when we are able to . . ."	Identify a central message in a story.	List relevant details from a story that support the central message.	Explain how the relevant details convey the central message.	Evaluate which relevant detail was the most important in conveying the central message of the story.
		List events in a story in order.	Compare relevant to irrelevant details.	
Context for learning: "Students will engage in their learning by . . ."	Students will engage in learning by reading *Charlotte's Web* through a "book club." The book club will have guiding questions for their discussions.			

RL.3.3 Describe characters in a story (e.g., their traits, motivations, or feelings) and explain how their actions contribute to the sequence of events.

	Subskills and Skills	Enabling Knowledge (information, facts) and Concepts
Learning Progression	Define	Character traits
	Identify	Character traits
	Define	Motivation
	Identify	Character motivations
	Identify	Character actions
	Identify	Story events
	Describe	Characters
	Explain	Connections between character actions and events
Understandings: "This is important to learn because . . ."	Just as every person is different, every character in a story is different.	
	Describing a character in detail brings a character to life.	
	Actions of characters, good or bad, drive the plot of the story.	

SOLO Level	Unistructural: One Idea	Multistructural: Many Ideas; No Connections Between Facts and Ideas	Relational: Connections Between Facts and Ideas	Extended Abstract: Generalize Learning and Apply to Different Contexts
Student-friendly learning intention: "We are learning to . . ."	Describe characters in a story and explain how what they do affects the story line.			
SOLO Verbs	Define	Describe	Explain	Predict
Success criteria: "We are successful when we are able to . . ."	Define what a character trait is. / Define what character motivation is.	Describe three characters.	Explain a character's actions and how his/her actions lead to the order of events.	Predict how the story would have changed if a character failed to take a critical action in the story.
Context for learning: "Students will engage in their learning by . . ."	Students will engage in learning by reading *Charlotte's Web* through a "book club." The book club will have guiding questions for their discussions.		Explain Charlotte's actions and how her actions lead to the order of events.	Recognizing Wilbur's character, predict what would have happened if he had been unable to convince Templeton to retrieve Charlotte's egg sac before leaving the fair.

W.3.1 Write opinion pieces on topics or texts, supporting a point of view with reasons.

  a. Introduce the topic or text they are writing about, state an opinion, and create an organizational structure that lists reasons.

  b. Provide reasons that support the opinion.

  c. Use linking words and phrases (e.g., because, therefore, since, for example) to connect opinion and reasons.

  d. Provide a concluding statement or section.

		Subskills and Skills	Enabling Knowledge (information, facts) and Concepts
		Define	Point of view, opinion
	Learning Progression	Distinguish	Fact from opinion
		Distinguish	An argument from an opinion
		Name	Organizational structures (list structures)
		Identify	Organizational structures of texts
		Name	Common linking words and phrases
		State	An opinion
		Identify	Supporting reasons
		Explain	Concluding statement or section
Understandings: "This is important to learn because . . ."		Writing is an important means of communicating.	
		Everyone has an opinion, but you need to support your opinion with sound information and facts.	
		How writing is organized depends on the style of writing.	
		Certain words serve different functions in writing.	

SOLO Level	Unistructural: One Idea	Multistructural: Many Ideas; No Connections Between Facts and Ideas	Relational: Connections Between Facts and Ideas	Extended Abstract: Generalize Learning and Apply to Different Contexts
Student-friendly learning intention: "We are learning to . . ."	Write opinion pieces on topics or texts and support your opinions with reasons.			
SOLO Verbs	Define/state	List and describe	Justify	Reflect
Success criteria: "We are successful when we are able to . . ."	Define point of view. Define opinion. State an opinion.	List and describe three types of organizational structures. List common linking words and phrases used when writing.	Justify your opinion. Apply an organizational structure and linking words.	Reflect on your opinion.
Context for learning: "Students will engage in their learning by . . ."	Write an opinion piece on your favorite *Charlotte's Web* character.			Reflect on your opinion of Templeton. Would it change if Templeton had not retrieved Charlotte's egg sac for Wilbur? Why or why not?

Performance Tasks

Performance Task Basics

Authentic task: Literary conversation
Role/position: Student/member of a book club
Audience: Other book club members
Motivating context: Your book club has decided to read E. B. White's *Charlotte's Web* in honor of the book's first publication 65 years ago. Each book club member will be assigned a main character from the book that he or she will closely follow throughout the reading of the book. Each book club member should be able to speak about his or her character and how the character is involved in the plot of the story.

Performance Task Student Directions

Your book club has decided to read E. B. White's *Charlotte's Web* in honor of the book's first publication 65 years ago. The book club has decided that each member must select a main character to follow closely throughout the book. Each book club member is responsible for the following:

Generic Scoring Guide, Book Club Conversation—Students Self-Assess the Book Club Group

Exceeds Success Criteria	*Meets Success Criteria*	*Approaching Meets Success Criteria*	*A Long Way From Meets Success Criteria*
Everything in Meets Success Criteria, Plus: • Students ask at least 3 deeper-level questions (relational or extended abstract).	• All students discuss the plot. • Each student is able to contribute to describing his or her focus character. • Each student is able to discuss the central message. • Students allow each other to complete their thoughts before speaking. • Students encourage each other to ask and answer questions.	At least 4 of 5 Meets Success Criteria have been attained.	1–3 of Meets Success Criteria have been attained.

- Be able to discuss the plot of the portion of the book assigned for that book club session.
- Be able to describe his or her selected character and the character's role in the actions of the story.
- Be able to discuss the central messages of the story.

Performance Task Basics

Authentic task: Written opinion
Role/position: Student
Audience: School librarian and community members via web page
Motivating context: Celebrating the 65th anniversary of the first publication of *Charlotte's Web*

Performance Task Student Directions

Mrs. Richards, the school librarian, is celebrating the 65th anniversary of the first publication of *Charlotte's Web*, by E. B. White, by asking students to write opinion pieces on their favorite *Charlotte's Web* character, including why those characters are their favorites. From all the written submissions, Mrs. Richards will determine the favorite character among the students, and five opinion pieces will be randomly selected each week of the month to be included on the school's web page for community members to read, along with a graph of the results of the choice of the favorite character at Oakridge Elementary. The guidelines for submitting an opinion piece are as follows:

- Introduce *Charlotte's Web*.
- State an opinion on your favorite character.
- Include a description of your favorite character and his or her role in the story's events.
- Use an organizational structure to explain your opinion.
- Justify your opinion with reasons.
- Use common linking words and phrases.
- Provide a concluding statement or section.

Task-Specific Scoring Guide

Exceeds Success Criteria	Meets Success Criteria	Approaching Meets Success Criteria	A Long Way From Meets Success Criteria
Everything in Meets Success Criteria, Plus: • Opinion is supported with more than 2 reasons. • Simple, compound, and complex sentences are used.	• Charlotte's Web is introduced. • Opinion of favorite character is stated. • Organizational structure lists reasons for opinion. • Opinion is supported with at least 2 reasons. • Common linking words and phrases are used. • There is a concluding statement or section.	At least 4 of 6 Meets Success Criteria have been attained.	1–3 of Meets Success Criteria have been attained.

Grade 11
Unit Planning Example

Teacher(s)/Team: 11th Grade West—Hicks, Gifford, Synokowski, Renniger, Bradford

Grade Level: 11th

Unit Title/Type (topical, thematic, skills-based): Foundations of American Government

Step 1. Identify the Primary Standards and Secondary Standards.

Unit Primary Standards

CE.2 The student will apply social science skills to understand the foundations of American constitutional government by

    a. explaining the fundamental principles of consent of the governed, limited government, rule of law, democracy, and representative government;

    b. examining and evaluating the impact of the Magna Carta, charters of the Virginia Company of London, the Virginia

Declaration of Rights, the Declaration of Independence, the Articles of Confederation, and the Virginia Statute for Religious Freedom on the Constitution of Virginia and the Constitution of the United States, including the Bill of Rights;

c. describing the purposes for the Constitution of the United States as stated in its Preamble; and

d. describing the procedures for amending the Constitution of Virginia and the Constitution of the United States.

CE.6 The student will apply social science skills to understand the American constitutional government at the national level by

b. explaining the principle of separation of powers and the operation of checks and balances.

Unit Secondary Standard

R.HS.11.12.2 Determine the central ideas or information of a primary or secondary source; provide an accurate summary that makes clear the relationships among the key details and ideas.

Step 2. Learning Progressions: What do you need to teach first? What follows? What comes next, etcetera? This includes subskills and enabling knowledge that is needed to attain the skills and knowledge within the standard, which are the end of the learning progression. Identify the understandings, etc.

CE.2 The student will apply social science skills to understand the foundations of American constitutional government by

a. explaining the fundamental principles of consent of the governed, limited government, rule of law, democracy, and representative government;

b. examining and evaluating the impact of the Magna Carta, charters of the Virginia Company of London, the Virginia Declaration of Rights, the Declaration of Independence, the Articles of Confederation, and the Virginia Statute for Religious Freedom on the Constitution of Virginia and the Constitution of the United States, including the Bill of Rights;

c. describing the purposes for the Constitution of the United States as stated in its Preamble;

d. describing the procedures for amending the Constitution of Virginia and the Constitution of the United States.

Learning Progression	Subskills and Skills	Enabling Knowledge (information, facts) and Concepts
	Define/describe	Consent of the governed
	Define/describe	Limited government
	Define/describe	Rule of law
	Define/describe	Representative government
	Define/describe	Democracy
Understandings: "This is important to learn because . . ."	American constitutional government is based on fundamental political principles that go back over two centuries.	
	These fundamental principles are present in our daily lives as U.S. citizens.	

Learning Progression	Subskills and Skills	Enabling Knowledge (information, facts) and Concepts
	Describe	Charters of the Virginia Company of London
	Describe	Virginia Declaration of Rights
	Describe	Declaration of Independence
	Describe	Articles of Confederation
	Describe	Virginia Statute for Religious Freedom
	Describe	Constitution of the United States (including purposes)
	Define	Bill of Rights
	List	Bill of Rights
	Describe	Constitution of Virginia
	List	Steps to amend the Virginia Constitution and the U.S. Constitution
Understandings: "This is important to learn because . . ."	American constitutional government is founded on concepts from earlier documents.	
	The U.S. Constitution is still the basis for interpreting laws and discussing issues.	
	The U.S. Constitution is founded on such strong concepts; there is good reason the process to amend it is challenging.	

CE.6 The student will apply social science skills to understand the American constitutional government at the national level by

    b. explaining the principle of separation of powers and the operation of checks and balances.

Learning Progression	Subskills and Skills	Enabling Knowledge (information, facts) and Concepts
	Describe	The three branches of government and their roles
	Define	Separation of powers
	Define	Checks and balances
Understandings: "This is important to learn because . . ."	Separation of powers is one means through which the Constitution prevents the branches from abusing power.	The system of checks and balances further curtails any one branch from exerting too much power.

SOLO Level	Unistructural: One Idea / Multistructural: Many Ideas; No Connections Between Facts and Ideas	Relational: Connections Between Facts and Ideas	Extended Abstract: Generalize Learning and Apply to Different Contexts
Student-friendly learning intention: "We are learning to . . ."	Explain the fundamental principles of American constitutional government.		
SOLO Verbs	Define/describe	Analyze	Predict
Success criteria: "We are successful when we are able to . . ."	Define each of the five fundamental principles of U.S. government (consent of the governed, limited government, rule of law, democracy, and representative government). Describe each of the five fundamental principles of U.S. government (consent of the governed, limited government, rule of law, democracy, and representative government).	Analyze the significance of the principles of government and their importance to today's government.	Predict how the American government would change if one of the principles did not exist.

(Continued)

(Continued)

SOLO verbs	Define/describe	Analyze	Predict
Context for learning: "Students will engage in their learning by . . ."	Creating an informational brochure (**Success criteria in bold will be included in the informational brochure.**)		

SOLO Level	Unistructural: One Idea / Multistructural: Many Ideas; No Connections Between Facts and Ideas	Relational: Connections Between Facts and Ideas	Extended Abstract: Generalize Learning and Apply to Different Contexts
Student-friendly learning intention: "We are learning to . . ."	Explain the significance of the charters of the Virginia Company of London, the Virginia Declaration of Rights, and the Virginia Statute for Religious Freedom.		
SOLO Verbs	Describe	Compare and contrast	Evaluate
Success criteria: "We are successful when we are able to . . ."	Describe the charters of the Virginia Company of London and their relationship to the Virginia Declaration of Rights.	Compare and contrast the Virginia Declaration of Rights with the U.S. Bill of Rights. **Explain the causes** Explain why the Virginia Statute for Religious Freedom is viewed as the foundation for the U.S. Bill of Rights.	Evaluate the Virginia Declaration of Rights and the Virginia Statute for Religious Freedom to determine which had more influence on the U.S. Bill of Rights and why.
Context for learning: "Students will engage in their learning by . . ."	Creating an informational brochure (**Success criteria in bold will NOT be included in the performance task informational brochure but will be formatively evaluated through another means.**)		

	Unistructural: One Idea Multistructural: Many Ideas; No Connections Between Facts and Ideas	Relational: Connections Between Facts and Ideas	Extended Abstract: Generalize Learning and Apply to Different Contexts
SOLO Level			
Student-friendly learning intention: "We are learning to . . ."	Explain the significance of the Declaration of Independence and the Articles of Confederation.		
SOLO Verbs	*List*	*Relate*	*Reflect*
Success criteria: "We are successful when we are able to . . ."	**List the six grievances against the king that are stated in the Declaration of Independence.**	**Relate the connections between the four components of the Declaration of Independence.**	**Reflect on the impacts of the Declaration of Independence on our lives today.**
	Describe	*Compare and Contrast*	*Evaluate*
	Describe the three key components of the Articles of Confederation.	**Compare and contrast the Virginia Declaration of Rights with the Declaration of Independence.**	Evaluate the impact of the Articles of Confederation on the U.S. Constitution.
Context for learning: "Students will engage in their learning by . . ."	Creating an informational brochure (Success criteria in bold will NOT be included in the performance task informational brochure but will be formatively evaluated through another means.)		

	Unistructural: One Idea / Multistructural: Many Ideas; No Connections Between Facts and Ideas	Relational: Connections Between Facts and Ideas	Extended Abstract: Generalize Learning and Apply to Different Contexts
SOLO Level			
Student-friendly learning intention: "We are learning to . . ."	Explain the significance of the U.S. Constitution and the Virginia Constitution.		
SOLO Verbs	*List*	*Analyze/explain Causes*	*Hypothesize*
	List the components of the U.S. Constitution. **List the components of the Virginia Constitution.**	Analyze the components of the US Constitution and why the US Constitution is organized the way it is.	Hypothesize how the U.S. government would function if Article 1, 2, or 3 of the U.S. Constitution were not included.
	Describe	*Compare and Contrast*	
Success criteria: "We are successful when we are able to . . ."	The functions of each of the components of the U.S. Constitution. **The functions of each of the components of the Virginia Constitution.**	**Compare and contrast the U.S. Constitution with the Virginia Constitution.**	
Context for learning: "Students will engage in their learning by . . ."	Creating an informational brochure **(Success criteria in bold will NOT be included in the performance task informational brochure but will be formatively evaluated through another means.)**		

SOLO Level	Unistructural: One Idea / Multistructural: Many Ideas; No Connections Between Facts and Ideas	Relational: Connections Between Facts and Ideas	Extended Abstract: Generalize Learning and Apply to Different Contexts
Student-friendly learning intention: "We are learning to . . ."	Identify the purposes of the Constitution of the United States and the procedure for amending the Constitution of Virginia and United States.		
SOLO Verbs	Describe	Justify	Hypothesize
Success criteria: "We are successful when we are able to . . ."	Describe the purposes of the Preamble to the U.S. Constitution.	Justify the U.S. Constitution amendment process. **Explain the causes.** Explain the causes behind the creation of the Bill of Rights.	Hypothesize the social and financial impact on the United States if the 21st Amendment were to be repealed.
Context for learning: "Students will engage in their learning by . . ."	Creating an informational brochure (**Success criteria in bold will NOT be included in the performance task informational brochure but will be formatively evaluated through another means.**)		

	Unistructural: One Idea / Multistructural: Many Ideas; No Connections Between Facts and Ideas	Relational: Connections Between Facts and Ideas	Extended Abstract: Generalize Learning and Apply to Different Contexts
SOLO Level			
Student-friendly learning intention: "We are learning to . . ."	Explain the principle of separation of powers and the operation of checks and balances as they relate to the government at the national level.		
SOLO Verbs	Name / Describe	Argue	Evaluate/formulate
Success criteria: "We are successful when we are able to . . ."	**Name the three branches of the U.S. government.** / Describe the functions of each of **the branches of government.**	**Argue why there are three branches of government and how the concept of checks and balances applies to each of the branches.**	**Evaluate the checks each branch of government has on the others and formulate a theory of which branch would abuse power more and why if the checks were not there.**
Context for learning: "Students will engage in their learning by . . ."	Creating an informational brochure **(Success criteria in bold will NOT be included in the performance task informational brochure but will be formatively evaluated through another means.)**		

198

Performance Task Basics

Authentic task: Information brochure
Role/position: National Archives Museum curator
Audience: Tourists
Motivating context: Preparing an informational brochure titled "The Foundations of American Government: Virginia's Role," to be distributed at the museum

Learning Intention Alignment

- We are learning to explain the fundamental principles of American constitutional government.
- We are learning to explain the significance of the charters of the Virginia Company of London, the Virginia Declaration of Rights, and the Virginia Statute for Religious Freedom.
- We are learning to identify the purposes of the Constitution of the United States and the procedure for amending the Constitution of Virginia and the U.S. Constitution.

Performance Task Student Directions

You are the curator at the National Archives Museum in Washington, D.C. The museum houses the Declaration of Independence, the U.S. Constitution, and the Bill of Rights. You have been charged with creating an informational brochure for tourists that will outline Virginia's role in the establishment of the foundations of the American government. Within the brochure you need to include the following sections:

- "Fundamental Principles"
- "Virginia's Role in American Constitutional Government"
- "The U.S. Constitution, Preamble, and Bill of Rights"

In the "Fundamental Principles" section:

- Define and describe the fundamental principles behind American constitutional government: consent of the governed, limited government, rule of law, democracy, and representative government.
- Analyze the significance of each of the principles, and to emphasize that significance, make a prediction of how the American government would change if one of the principles did not exist.

In "Virginia's Role in American Constitutional Government" section:

- Describe the charters of the Virginia Company of London and their relationship to the Virginia Declaration of Rights.
- Compare and contrast the Virginia Declaration of Rights with the U.S. Bill of Rights.
- Explain why the Virginia Statute for Religious Freedom is viewed as the foundation for the U.S. Bill of Rights.
- Evaluate the Virginia Declaration of Rights and the Virginia Statute for Religious Freedom to determine which had more influence on the U.S. Bill of Rights and why.

In the "U.S. Constitution, Preamble, and Bill of Rights" section:

- Describe the goals and purposes of the Preamble to the U.S. Constitution.
- Describe the function of each of the components of the U.S. Constitution.
- Analyze the components of the U.S. Constitution and explain why the Constitution is organized the way it is.
- Create a visual of the process of how the U.S. Constitution can be amended and justify the amendment process.
- Explain the causes behind the creation of the Bill of Rights.
- Hypothesize how the U.S. government would function if Article 1, 2, or 3 were not included in the U.S. Constitution. Select only one article.
- Hypothesize the social and financial impact on the United States if the 21st Amendment were repealed.

As you create the brochure, try to do the following:

- Write accurate information.
- Apply organizational structures as needed to written responses.
- Use section headings to aid comprehension.
- Use effects such as varied fonts and font sizes, shading, graphics, and pictures to enhance reader comprehension and visual appeal.

Scoring Guide

Exceeds Success Criteria	Meets Success Criteria	Approaching Meets Success Criteria	A Long Way From Meets Success Criteria
Everything in Meets Success Criteria, Plus: • Organizational structures fit the type of writing being applied in each section. • Section headings are used to aid comprehension. • Effects such as varied fonts, shading, graphics, and pictures are used to enhance comprehension and visual appeal.	**The brochure includes:** • The three required sections • Accurate description of the four fundamental principles • Analysis of the significance of each of the principles • A prediction of how the American government would change if one of the principles did not exist to support the analysis • Accurate description of the charters of the Virginia Company of London and their relationship to the Virginia Declaration of Rights • Accurate explanation of why the Virginia Statute for Religious Freedom is viewed as the foundation for the U.S. Bill of Rights • Evaluation of the Virginia Declaration of Rights and the Virginia Statute for Religious Freedom to determine which had more influence on the U.S. Bill of Rights and why • Accurate description of the purposes of the Preamble to the U.S. Constitution • Accurate description of the functions of the components of the U.S. Constitution • Analysis of the components of the U.S. Constitution and an explanation of why they are organized the way they are • Hypothesis of how the U.S. government would function if Article 1, 2, or 3 were not included in the U.S. Constitution (only one article selected) • Hypothesis of the social and financial impact on the United States if the 21st Amendment were to be repealed • Accurate visual representation of the process of how the U.S. Constitution can be amended • Accurate explanation of the causes behind the creation of the Bill of Rights	At least 6–10 Meets Success Criteria have been attained.	1–5 of Meets Success Criteria have been attained.

> This is written as a holistic scoring guide. It could easily be written as an analytical scoring guide, which would be preferred for greater feedback. There would be a dimension for each of the sections of the brochure and the criteria could be more specific.

Appendix 3

Combined List:
SOLO and NCEA Verbs

Unistructural	Multistructural	Relational	Extended Abstract
Identify	Combine	Analyze	Create
Name	Describe	Apply	Formulate
Follow a simple	Enumerate	Argue	Generate
procedure	Perform serial	Compare/	Hypothesize
Define	skills	contrast	Reflect
Draw	List	Criticize	Theorize
Find	Outline	Explain causes	Predict
Label	Follow an	Relate	Evacuate
Match	algorithm	Justify	Prove
		Sequence	Plan
		Classify	Justify
		Explain effects	Argue
		Form an analogy	Compose
		Organize	Prioritize
		Distinguish	Design
		Interview	Construct
		Question	Perform

Note: The verbs *argue* and *justify* appear in both the relational and extended abstract levels. They serve as guides, since formulating arguments and justifications requires students to respond at deeper levels of understanding. If a student goes beyond relating the information when arguing, justifying, or incorporating prior knowledge and other information, the response is at the extended abstract level.

Appendix 4

Unit Planning Template: Ideas for Products and Performances

The key to choosing products and performances for students' learning experiences is to contemplate the products and performances of real-world people working in their everyday jobs and occupations. Following is a list of some of the many kinds of products and performances from which you might choose, along with a few of the jobs, occupations, and businesses associated with them.

Products and Performances	Jobs, Occupations, Businesses
Poems	Authors (books, magazines, newspapers, journals)
Short stories, fables, myths, or literature of other genres	Authors (children's literature, adult literature)
Arguments	Lawyers, politicians, scientists
Scripts	Playwrights, screenwriters, television writers
Letters (business, friendly)	Businesspersons, students
Informational reports	Scientists (geologists, marine biologists, botanists, meteorologists, and so on), political lobbyists, museum curators, nutritionists
Informational articles	Authors (magazines, newspapers, journals)

(Continued)

(Continued)

Products and Performances	Jobs, Occupations, Businesses
Informational brochures	Marketing firms, advertising agencies, chambers of commerce, tourist organizations, zoos, aquariums, national parks, museums
Editorials	Citizens (newspapers, magazines, journals)
Critiques or reviews	Critics for topic-specific magazines (movie review for *Entertainment Weekly*, book review in the *New Yorker*), critics for newspapers
Business plans	Entrepreneurs
Literary analyses	Authors (magazines, newspapers, journals)
Observation logs, with summaries and hypotheses	Scientists, nutritionists
Cartoons	Artists, political commentators, authors
Speeches	Speechwriters (for politicians, lobbyists, business executives)
Web pages	Web designers, students
Videos	Advertising agencies, marketing firms, documentary directors
Oral presentations	Informational speakers, politicians
Excel spreadsheets	Accountants, survey analysts
Artworks (paintings, drawings, sculptures)	Artists, graphic designers, interior designers, advertising agencies
Models	Engineers, inventors, model makers, Lego designers
Graphs	Political analysts, financial analysts, scientists
Experiments	Scientists, social scientists
Theater performances	Actors, students
Musical performances	Musicians, students

Appendix 5

Implementation Success Action Plan: Guidelines

No matter the level (classroom, grade, department, building, or district), the successful implementation of any educational initiative relies on the establishment of an implementation success action plan to guide implementation efforts and keep the endeavor on track. Failure to achieve implementation at deep levels tends to be the downfall for most initiatives, preventing them from improving student achievement and growth as much as they could.

The starting point for developing an implementation success action plan is to complete a "vision versus reality" activity such as the one presented in Appendix 7. Once you have articulated your vision and completed an honest assessment of the reality, the gap between where you are and where you want to be will determine the steps you need to take to close the gap.

The implementation success action plan recommended here (see the template in Appendix 8) follows a format that includes four major components: front matter, implementation strategies, implementation action steps, and a monitoring and evaluation plan. Each component should be completed no matter the level (classroom, grade, department, building, or district) on which the plan will be utilized.

The front matter identifies the project title, the project team, and the project lead. The number of people on the team depends on the level for which the plan is being developed, but bear in mind that managing teams of eight or more can become a bit unwieldy. The front matter also includes a statement of the district mission as well as the district goal the project is targeting. In the case of implementing performance tasks, the intent is to see improvement in student achievement. A building goal that is aligned to the district goal may be stated, and if you are focusing on classroom, grade-level, or department implementation, you can add another section for that level's goal.

The implementation strategies section of the plan lists two to four overarching strategies that will close the gap between reality and vision and keep it closed. These may be strategies such as providing professional development and ongoing support, building leadership capacity among staff, improving communication, or securing supplies and materials. The action steps that are listed are related to the strategies established. You may want to consider creating the action steps first and then determining the emerging themes among the steps, such as professional development or communication. There are no "implementation success action plan police"—no hard-and-fast rules say that you have to create the strategies before the action steps.

The action steps take into consideration all the minor details that might get overlooked as implementation is being rolled out. Additionally, there is no harm done if you decide to change, add, or delete any action steps as you are proceeding through them. The implementation success action plan should be considered a living document. The plan template includes spaces for noting which strategies are supported by the action steps, as well as who is responsible for each action step and the due date of the step. The final column on the template is space for comments and notes about next steps. This column is filled in after the action step is completed. Sometimes the completion of one action step generates another step, or you may need to note a reminder about a particular step. The key thing to remember is that the steps are intended to close the gap between reality and vision.

When determining specific action steps, it is useful to list them in the implementation success action plan in the order in which they need to be completed; also, no action should be considered too small to be included. The goal is to be proactive rather than just go from action to action.

Here are a few guidelines to follow and questions team members should ask while developing action steps:

- Include initial professional development.
- Include ongoing professional development.
- Include parental engagement.
- Remember the importance of using consistent language among teachers, students, and parents.

- What will make it easier for teachers, so that from day one they can start implementation?
- Do any guidelines for implementation need to be developed?
- Do any materials need to be ordered or bought?
- Does anything need to be laminated?
- If you think there will be pushback, are there actions you can take to help mitigate that?
- How can successes and challenges be shared to keep the implementation moving forward?
- How can data (not including the names of teachers or students) be made transparent to all staff, students, and parents?
- Do timelines for data collection need to be developed?
- How will successes be celebrated?

The final component of the implementation success action plan is the monitoring and evaluation plan, which identifies the kinds of data to be collected on a regular basis (typically monthly, but that may not apply to all data collection items, as you can see in the example plan in Appendix 6). There are two types of data, cause data and effect data, and you need both to see the whole picture. The purpose of collecting both types of data monthly (when possible) is so that you can determine the impacts of the cause data on the effect data and adjust the implementation strategies and action steps if they are not having the desired results. Most educators at the classroom, school, and district levels are more familiar with effect data, as these are the data that students produce—for example, the percentage of students who attain a passing score on an assessment, the percentage of students present every day of the month, or the percentage of students with no discipline referrals each month. On the other side of the coin are cause data: data collected on specified teacher/leader actions. So, the percentage of students passing an assessment could be related to the number of performance tasks completed during the month; the number of students present could also be related to the number of performance tasks completed in a month or the number of one-on-one conferences each teacher had with individual students to discuss progress and feedback. Discipline referrals could also be related to the number of performance tasks in a month, as well as the number of teachers who established and practiced classroom procedures during performance tasks. The monitoring and evaluation plan includes due dates for data collection and specifies who is responsible for collecting the data. Once the details of data collection have been determined, the implementation team may find it necessary to go back to the list of action steps to incorporate additional steps related to data collection sheets, explanations of data collection for teachers, and so on.

Once the data are collected, they should be graphed to show the connections between causes and effects. Are the teachers who are using the most performance tasks for instructional purposes versus assessment purposes getting the higher student scores on assessments? Are behaviors better in the classrooms of those teachers? Has attendance improved in those classes? Such benefits are the intended outcomes of performance tasks, which have the potential to improve student learning, resulting in greater student achievement, engagement, and motivation.

Appendix 6

Implementation Success Action Plan: Example

Project Title: Development of real-world performance tasks to measure attainment of CCSS **Project Members:** Susan, Jean, Wendy, Monica, Robert, Alyssa, Pam, and Robin **Project Manager:** Robin
District Mission: Recognizing the value of each individual, and building upon our commitment to excellence, the Rodney School District is dedicated to the mission of preparing students for a successful, productive, and purposeful life in a diverse, global community by: Providing quality educational opportunities for all students; and Promoting caring attitudes through the school community. **District Goal:** Meet or exceed the adequate yearly progress (AYP) targets and state progress determination (SPD) goals in all core content areas in the school accountability system, with emphasis on the special education cell.

Building Goal: What is the building goal, aligned with the district goal above, that the project is aimed at achieving?

To increase academic proficiency in reading for grades 3–5 as measured by the SBAC in June 2018. Specifically, increase grade 3 from ____% to ____%, grade 4 from ____% to ____%, and grade 5 from ____% to ____%. To increase academic proficiency in reading for special education students in grades 3–5, as measured by the SBAC in June 2018. Specifically, increase grade 3 from ___% to ___%, grade 4 from ___% to ___%, and grade 5 from ____% to ____%.

Implementation Success Action Plan Strategies: Reflect on your vision and reality activity. What strategies will it take to close the gap? Identify the overarching strategies the project team will utilize to fully implement the project and achieve the identified school building goal. These are the main components that will move the project forward and close the gap between the VISION of the project and the current REALITY. These are the BIG PICTURE actions the project team will put in place.

1. Establish a vision and communicate the vision for the implementation of performance tasks.
2. Build leadership capacity.
3. Provide initial and ongoing professional development and support.

Project Implementation Action Steps: Identify the specific action steps you will take to achieve the Big Picture strategies, what strategies they support, the team member(s) accountable for accomplishing the action steps, and when the action steps need to be completed. Sometimes an action step has its own subset of action steps; these can be listed below the action step.

Project Implementation Action Steps	Strategy	Accountable Project Team Member(s)	Due Date	Other Comments; Next Steps
Create an online survey on performance tasks for teachers and administrators to take.	1	Monica, Wendy, Jean, Robert	May 23, 2017	
Create an online student engagement survey on performance tasks.	1	Monica, Wendy, Jean, Robert	May 23, 2017	
Identify and read resources to support the implementation of authentic performance tasks.	1	Susan, Alyssa, Robin, Pam	May 31, 2017	
Create a vision for the implementation of authentic performance tasks; share the vision with staff.	1	Project team	June 6 and 10, 2017	
Create criteria and expectations for teacher leaders who will attend seminar and certification on developing performance tasks.	2	Susan, Wendy, Robin, Robert	June 10, 2017	

Create interview questions for interested teacher leaders.	2	Susan, Wendy, Robin, Robert	June 10, 2017	
Interview teachers and select 5 teacher leaders to attend seminar and certification.	2	Susan, Wendy, Robin, Robert	June 12, 2017	
Make arrangements for teachers and administrators to attend seminar and certification. • Enroll in seminar and certification. • Arrange for 2 district vehicles. • Get approval for team-building dinner.	2, 3	Jean	June 25, 2017	
Attend seminar on performance tasks.	2, 3	Project team	July 12–13, 2017	
Attend certification training on performance tasks.	2, 3	Project team	August 1–3, 2017	
Create a plan to provide building professional development by the certified teachers.	2, 3	Project team	August 4, 2017	
Establish guidelines for grade-level teams on the number of performance assessments/tasks to be developed and implemented over the 2017–15 school year.	1, 3	Project team	August 4, 2017	
Provide professional development to the building.	2, 3	Robin, Wendy, Pam—main presenters; project team members supporting participants	August 28, 2017	Have multipurpose room set up on August 27; projector, screen

(Continued)

(Continued)

Project Implementation Action Steps	Strategy	Accountable Project Team Member(s)	Due Date	Other Comments; Next Steps
Arrange for biweekly meetings of the performance task team to monitor progress and discuss additional resources and support needed for the grade levels.	2, 3	Susan	August 30, 2017	
Have a celebration for teachers to share their successes and challenges. • Order cupcakes for the celebration. • Have Dunkin Donuts coffee and tea available along with water. • Send invitations to district (superintendent, director of curriculum, board president).	1, 2	Pam, Alyssa, Wendy	November 10, 2017	
Plan for a performance task showcase night for parents. • Create flyer or postcard to send home (maybe developed by students in a performance task). • Arrange for student/teacher presentations or panel discussion.	1, 3	Monique, Jean, Pam, Robert	December 14, 2017	
Host showcase night.	1, 2	Susan, Robin	January 12, 2017	

Monitoring and Evaluation Plan: What data will be collected to monitor and evaluate the level of success of your plan and allow you to make adjustments as needed? Cause data are the data collected on adult actions; effect data are the data produced by students.

Data (cause and effect)	Dates Collected								Accountable Project Team Member(s)	Other Comments; Next Steps
Professional development, initial and ongoing, provided by certified staff during PLCs	Sept. 30	Oct. 30	Nov. 30	Jan. 30	Feb. 28	Mar. 30		May 30	Robin, Jean	
Number of performance tasks created and implemented by teachers	Sept. 30	Oct. 30	Nov. 30	Jan. 30	Feb. 28	Mar. 30	Apr. 30	May 30	Wendy, Robert	
Proficiency of students on performance tasks	Sept. 30	Oct. 30	Nov. 30	Jan. 30	Feb. 28	Mar. 30	Apr. 30	May 30	Wendy, Robert	
Proficiency of students on quarterly district writing prompts	Oct. 15	Jan. 15	Mar. 15	June 15					Susan, Pam	
Online teacher survey	June 15								Monique	
Online student engagement survey	Sept. 30			Jan. 30				May 30	Alyssa, Monique	

Appendix 7

Implementation Success Action Plan: Vision Versus Reality

VISION: If your project is put into place, what will it look like, sound like, and feel like for all stakeholders involved (teachers, students, parents, administrators, community members, and others)?

What will it look like in the school building when the project is fully implemented?	What will it sound like in the school building when the project is fully implemented? What will stakeholders be saying, and how will they be saying it?	What will it feel like in the building when the project is fully implemented? What culture and climate characteristics will the school be exuding?

REALITY: What is the present status of the project you want to put in place? What does it currently look like, sound like, and feel like for all stakeholders involved (teachers, students, parents, administrators, community members, and others)?

What does it currently look like in the school building with respect to the project?	What does it currently sound like in the school building with respect to the project? What are stakeholders saying, and how are they saying it?	What does it currently feel like in the building with respect to the project? What culture and climate characteristics is the school exuding?

Appendix 8

Implementation Success Action Plan: Template

Project Title: _____

Project Members: _____

Project Manager: _____

District Mission:

District Goal:

Building Goal Aligned With District Goal: _____

Aligned Inquiry Statement ("If . . . , then"):

Implementation Success Action Plan Strategies: Reflect on your vision and reality activity. What overarching strategies (professional development, building leadership capacity, effective two-way communication, and so on) will it take to close the gap between reality and vision?

Strategy 1: _____

_____

Strategy 2: _____

_____

Strategy 3: _____

_____

Strategy 4: _____

_____

Project Implementation Action Steps: Identify the specific action steps you will take to achieve the strategies, what strategies they support, the team member(s) accountable for accomplishing the action steps, and when the action steps need to be completed. Sometimes an action step has its own subset of action steps; these can be listed below the action step.

Project Implementation Action Steps	Strategy	Accountable Project Team Member(s)	Due Date	Materials and/or Resources Needed	Other Comments; Next Steps

(Continued)

(Continued)

Monitoring and Evaluation Plan: What data (cause and effect) will be collected as evidence of the project's effectiveness and allow the project team to make adjustments as needed?

Measurable Evidence: Effect Data

Effect Data	Dates Collected									Accountable Project Team Member(s)	Other Comments; Next Steps

(Continued)

(Continued)

Measurable Evidence: Cause Data

Cause Data	Dates Collected									Accountable Project Team Member(s)	Other Comments; Next Steps

References

Achieve. (2015, July). *The role of learning progressions in competency-based pathways*. Washington, DC: Author. Retrieved from http://www.achieve.org/files/Achieve-LearningProgressionsinCBP.pdf

Ainsworth, L. (2003). *"Unwrapping" the standards: A simple process to make standards manageable*. Englewood, CO: Advanced Learning Press.

Ainsworth, L. (2010). *Rigorous curriculum design: How to create curricular units of study that align standards, instruction, and assessment*. Englewood, CO: Lead + Learn Press.

Ainsworth, L. (2015). *Common formative assessments 2.0: How teacher teams intentionally align standards, instruction, and assessment*. Thousand Oaks, CA: Corwin.

Barber, M., Rodriguez, N., & Artis, E. (2016). *Deliverology in practice: How education leaders are improving student outcomes*. Thousand Oaks, CA: Corwin.

Biggs, J. B. (n.d.). SOLO taxonomy. Retrieved from Johnbiggs.com.au

Biggs, J. B., & Collis, K. F. (1982). *Evaluating the quality of learning: The SOLO taxonomy (structure of the observed learning outcome)*. New York, NY: Academic Press.

Black, P., & Wiliam, D. (1998). Assessment and classroom learning. *Assessment in Education: Principles, Policy & Practice, 5*(1), 7–74.

Brookhart, S. M. (2013). *How to create and use rubrics for formative assessment and grading*. Alexandria, VA: Association for Supervision and Curriculum Development.

Brookhart, S. M. (2015). *Performance assessment: Showing what students know and can do*. West Palm Beach, FL: Learning Sciences International.

Burke, K. (2011). *From standards to rubrics in six steps: Tools for assessing student learning* (3rd ed.). Thousand Oaks, CA: Corwin.

Busteed, B. (2013, January 7). The school cliff: Student engagement drops with each school year. Gallup. Retrieved from http://www.gallup.com/opinion/gallup/170525/school-cliff-student-engagement-drops-school-year.aspx

Clarke, S. (2001). *Unlocking formative assessment*. London: Hodder & Stoughton.

Clarke, S. (2008). *Active learning through formative assessment*. London, England: Hodder Education.

Cohen, P. (1995). Designing performance assessment tasks. *Education Update, 37*(6), 1, 4–5, 8.

Common Core State Standards Initiative. (n.d.). About the standards. Retrieved from http://www.corestandards.org

Common Core State Standards Initiative. (2010a). *Common Core State Standards for English Language Arts and Literacy in History/Social Studies, Science, and Technical Subjects.* Retrieved from http://www.corestandards.org/wp-content/uploads/ELA_Standards1.pdf

Common Core State Standards Initiative. (2010b). *Common Core State Standards for Mathematics.* Retrieved from http://www.corestandards.org/wp-content/uploads/Math_Standards1.pdf

Darling-Hammond, L. (2008). *Powerful learning: What we know about teaching for understanding.* San Francisco, CA: Jossey-Bass.

Darling-Hammond, L. (2014, January/February). Testing to, and beyond, the Common Core. *Principal, 93*(3), 8–12.

Darling-Hammond, L., & Adamson, F. (2010). *Beyond basic skills: The role of performance assessment in achieving 21st century standards of learning.* Stanford, CA: Stanford Center for Opportunity Policy in Education, Stanford University.

Darling-Hammond, L., & Adamson, F. (2014). *Beyond the bubble test: How performance assessments support 21st century learning.* San Francisco, CA: Jossey-Bass.

Davies, A. (2007). Involving students in the classroom assessment process. In D. Reeves (Ed.), *Ahead of the curve: The power of assessment to transform teaching and learning* (pp. 31–57). Bloomington, IN: Solution Tree Press.

Education Northwest. (2014, May). 6+1 Trait rubrics. Retrieved from http://educationnorthwest.org/traits/traits-rubrics

Emmer, E. T., Evertson, C. M., & Worsham, M. E. (2006). *Classroom management for middle and high school teachers* (7th ed.). Boston, MA: Pearson.

Erickson, H. L. (2007). *Concept-based curriculum and instruction for the thinking classroom.* Thousand Oaks, CA: Corwin.

Evertson, C. M., Emmer, E. T., & Worsham, M. E. (2006). *Classroom management for elementary teachers* (7th ed.). Boston, MA: Pearson.

Flach, T. (2011). *Engaging students through performance assessment: Creating performance tasks to monitor student learning.* Englewood, CO: Advanced Learning Press.

Frey, N., Fisher, D., & Everlove, S. (2009). *Productive group work: How to engage students, build teamwork, and promote understanding.* Alexandria, VA: Association for Supervision and Curriculum Development.

Fullan, M., & Langworthy, M. (2014). *A rich seam: How new pedagogies find deep learning.* London, England: Pearson.

Gewertz, C. (2015, August 5). N.Y.C. school aims for "authentic," not standardized, tests. *Education Week,* p. 8.

Glass, K. T. (2013). *Mapping comprehensive units to the ELA Common Core standards 6–12.* Thousand Oaks, CA: Corwin.

Gonchar, M. (2015, February 5). 301 prompts for argumentative writing. *New York Times,* Learning Network blog. Retrieved from http://learning.blogs.nytimes.com/2015/02/05/301-prompts-for-argumentative-writing

Hall, G. E., & Hord, S. M. (2011). *Implementing change: Patterns, principles, and potholes* (3rd ed.). Boston, MA: Pearson.

Hattie, J. (2009). *Visible learning: A synthesis of over 800 meta-analyses relating to achievement.* New York, NY: Routledge.

Hattie, J. (2012). *Visible learning for teachers: Maximizing impact on learning.* New York, NY: Routledge.

Hattie, J., & Timperley, H. (2007). The power of feedback. *Review of Educational Research, 77*(1), 81–112.

Hattie, J., & Yates, G. (2014). *Visible learning and the science of how we learn.* New York, NY: Routledge.

Heitin, L. (2015, May 5). Districts out ahead of states in adopting science standards. *Education Week.* Retrieved from http://www.edweek.org/ew/articles/2015/05/06/districts-out-ahead-of-states-in-adopting.html?qs=heitin+may+6,+2015

Heritage, M. (2010). *Formative assessment: Making it happen in the classroom.* Thousand Oaks, CA: Corwin.

Hess, K. (2008). *Developing and using learning progressions as a schema for measuring progress.* National Center for Assessment. Retrieved from http://www.nciea.org/publication_PDFs/CCSSO2_KH08.pdf

Hook, P., & Mills, J. (2011). *SOLO taxonomy: A guide for schools,* book 1, *A common language of learning* (Kindle ed.). Invercargill, New Zealand: Essential Resources Educational Publishers.

Illinois Social Science Standards Revision Task Force. (2015, May). Illinois Social Science Standards recommendations. Retrieved from http://www.isbe.state.il.us/ils/social_science/standards.htm

Jones, B. R. (2014). *The focus model: Systematic school improvement for all schools.* Thousand Oaks, CA: Corwin.

Klein, A. (2015, April 10). No Child Left Behind: An overview. *Education Week.* Retrieved from http://www.edweek.org/ew/section/multimedia/no-child-left-behind-overview-definition-summary.html

Klein, A. (2016, January 6). New law, fresh challenges. *Education Week,* pp. 10–12.

Knight, J. (2013). *High-impact instruction: A framework for great teaching.* Thousand Oaks, CA: Corwin.

Krownapple, J. (2015, December 3). *Equity leaders must work themselves out of a job: What collective efficacy has to do with educational equity.* Corwin Connect. Retrieved from http://corwin-connect.com/2015/12/equity-leaders-must-work-themselves-out-of-a-job-what-collective-efficacy-has-to-do-with-educational-equity

Lanning, L. A. (2013). *Designing a concept-based curriculum for English language arts.* Thousand Oaks, CA: Corwin.

Martin, S. (2011). *Using SOLO as a framework for teaching: A case study in maximizing achievement in science* (Kindle ed.). Invercargill, New Zealand: Essential Resources Educational Publishers.

Martin-Kniep, G. O. (2000). *Becoming a better teacher: Eight innovations that work.* Alexandria, VA: Association for Supervision and Curriculum Development.

Martin-Kniep, G. O. (2011). *Leveraging the Common Core standards with authentic assessments.* Learner-Centered Initiatives. Retrieved from http://www.lciltd.org/images/stories/pdf-files/Leveraging_the_Common_Core_Standards_LCI.pdf

Marzano, R. J. (with Marzano, J. S., & Pickering, D. J.). (2003). *Classroom management that works: Research-based strategies for every teacher.* Alexandria, VA: Association for Supervision and Curriculum Development.

Masters, G., & Forster, M. (1996). *Developmental assessment: Assessment resource kit.* Melbourne: Australian Council for Educational Research.

McTighe, J. (2015, April 14). Performance Task Blog Series #1—What is a performance task? Jay McTighe & Associates, Educational Counseling. Retrieved from http://jaymctighe.com/2015/04/what-is-a-performance-task

Measured Progress/ETS Collaborative. (2012, April 16). *Smarter Balanced Assessment Consortium: Performance task specifications.* Retrieved from https://www.smarterbalanced.org/wp-content/uploads/2015/08/PerformanceTasksSpecifications.pdf

Moon, T. R., Brighton, C. M., Callahan, C. M., & Robinson, A. (2005). Development of authentic assessments for the middle school classroom. *Journal of Secondary Gifted Education, 16*(2–3), 119–133.

National Commission on Excellence in Education. (1983). *A nation at risk.* Retrieved from http://www2.ed.gov/pubs/NatAtRisk/risk.html

National Conference of State Legislatures. (n.d.). *Summary of Every Student Succeeds Act, legislation reauthorizing the Elementary and Secondary Education Act.* Retrieved from http://www.ncsl.org/documents/educ/ESSA_summary_NCSL.pdf

National Research Council. (2006). *Systems for state science assessment.* Committee on Test Design for K–12 Science Achievement, M. R. Wilson and M. W. Bertenthal, eds. Washington, DC: National Academies Press. Retrieved from http://www.nap.edu/download.php?record_id=11312#

Partnership for Assessment of Readiness for College and Careers. (n.d.). Glossary of terms: Clarifying language and terms. Retrieved from http://www.parcconline.org/resources/parent-resources/glossary-of-terms

Partnership for 21st Century Learning. (2015). *P21 framework definitions.* Retrieved from http://www.p21.org/storage/documents/docs/P21_Framework_Definitions_New_Logo_2015.pdf

Pfeffer, J., & Sutton, R. I. (2000). *The knowing-doing gap: How smart companies turn knowledge into action.* Boston, MA: Harvard Business School Press.

Popham, W. J. (2003). *Test better, teach better: The instructional role of assessment.* Alexandria, VA: Association for Supervision and Curriculum Development.

Popham, W. J. (2008). *Transformative assessment.* Alexandria, VA: Association for Supervision and Curriculum Development.

Quaglia, R. J., & Corso, M. J. (2014). *Student voice: The instrument of change.* Thousand Oaks, CA: Corwin.

Reeves, D. B. (2004). *Making standards work: How to implement standards-based assessments in the classroom, school, and district* (3rd ed.). Englewood, CO: Advanced Learning Press.

Sadler, D. R. (1989). Formative assessment and the design of instructional systems. *Instructional Science, 18,* 119–144.

Stiggins, R. (2006). *Balanced assessment: Redefining excellence in assessment.* Portland, OR: Educational Testing Service.

Stiggins, R. (2014). *Revolutionize assessment: Empower students, inspire learning.* Thousand Oaks, CA: Corwin.

Stronge, J. H. (2007). *Qualities of effective teachers* (2nd ed.). Alexandria, VA: Association for Supervision and Curriculum Development.

Tate, M. L. (2014). *Shouting won't grow dendrites.* Thousand Oaks, CA: Corwin.

U.S. Department of Education. (n.d.). Race to the Top Fund: Program description. Retrieved from http://www2.ed.gov/programs/racetothetop/index.html

Visible Learning[plus]. (n.d.-a). *Building and developing visible learners workbook.* Thousand Oaks, CA: Corwin.

Visible Learning[plus]. (n.d.-b). *Foundation workbook.* Thousand Oaks, CA: Corwin.

White House, Office of the Press Secretary. (2015, December 2). Fact sheet: Congress acts to fix No Child Left Behind. Retrieved from https://www.whitehouse.gov/the-press-office/2015/12/03/fact-sheet-congress-acts-fix-no-child-left-behind

Wiggins, G., & McTighe, J. (2005). *Understanding by design* (2nd ed.). Alexandria, VA: Association for Supervision and Curriculum Development.

Yazzie-Mintz, E. (2010). *Charting the path from engagement to achievement: A report on the 2009 High School Survey of Student Engagement.* Bloomington: Center for Evaluation & Education Policy, Indiana University.

Index